YOUR BUSINESS, YOUR LIFE

Reap the Rewards

PETER GIALOURIS

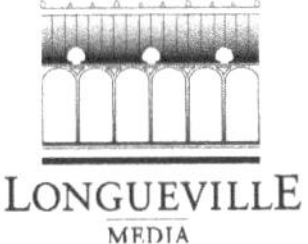

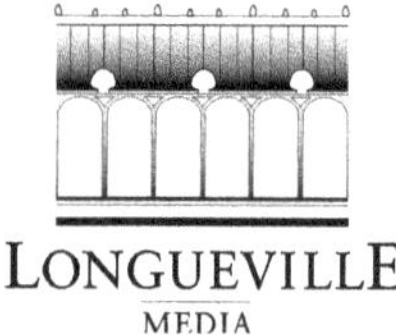

First published by Longueville Media for
Peter Gialouris, 2017

Longueville Media
PO Box 205
Haberfield NSW 2045
www.longuevillemedia.com.au
T. +61 2 9362 8441

A CIP catalogue record for this book is available from the National Library of
Australia website: www.nla.gov.au

ISBN: 978-0-9876213-3-7
eBook: 978-0-9876213-6-8

Disclaimer

The material in this book is of a general nature and is provided for information purposes only. It has been prepared without taking account of your objectives, financial situation or needs and therefore before acting upon the information contained in this publication you should consider its appropriateness with regard to your objectives, financial situation and needs. Always obtain professional advice from a qualified specialist in this area, such as an accountant, lawyer or a certified financial planner, before proceeding.

The information provided in this book, including references to relevant laws, regulations and rates was accurate at the time of writing. These can and do change over time and these changes may impact on the strategies and actions outlined herein.

References to income and growth rates are based on projected future performance, and are intended only as a guide to likely returns and should be treated as such.

Always remember that past performance is not a reliable indicator of future performance.

Acknowledgements

To Andrew Griffiths, Glen Carlson and the Dent Team, thank you for the motivation and guidance to write this book.

To David Longfield, Siobhan Gallagher and the Longueville Media Team, thank you for helping craft the book and making it a reality.

To my family and friends, especially Elizabeth, Daniel, Emma, Will and Josh, thank you for encouraging me and putting up with it all. You are my Pillars – my special people.

Thank you also to everyone, who over the years and in their own way, has helped me and has contributed to this book. To Lifespan Financial Planning for the use of their technical material and to my wonderful clients for walking the talk.

CONTENTS

Introduction.. i

Section 1. The Big Picture.. 1
1   The 6 Pillars of Financial Success 3
2   Top Challenges for Small Businesses 14

Section 2. Your Business, Your Plan 21
3   The Results Review 22
4   Your Business Plan 31
5   Your Personal Financial Plan 47

Section 3. Applying CADTRE: Your 6 Pillars for Financial Success... 64
6   C: Harnessing Cash Flow... 66
7   A: Asset Building and Preservation 79
     Your Investment Plan 85
8   D: Debt Management 105
9   T: Tax Strategies.. 111
10   R: Risk, Protecting Your Downside............................ 121
11   E: Estate and Succession Planning 136

Section 4. Gain an Edge 150
12   The Value of Professional Advice 151
13   Go from a Maze to Amazing!..................................... 158

Appendices
A: Short Form Business and Personal Financial Plan................. 160
B: Business and Investment Structures........................... 178
C: Crafting an Investment Strategy................................ 181

Recommended Reading.. 187

About the Author... 188

Introduction

**Every owner should aim to become
financially independent of their business.**

The goal is to ensure your business works for you as much as you work for your business.

Are you shaking your head in amusement or disbelief? As a small business owner, you are often so immersed in your business that you don't take the time necessary to ensure your money and efforts work for you. Your business is personal. It's a big part of who you are, what you represent, and often what you stand for.

Like most small business owners, you possess the expertise and talent to work *in* your business. That's generally why you started your business and why you have stayed in business. And why it is so important to keep developing and honing your skills.

Working *on* the business, and *beyond* the business, often requires different knowledge and sets of skills. And just like you can't do it all yourself *in* the business, neither can you do everything singlehandedly when working *on* your business and *beyond* it (that is, on your personal finances). No one can juggle all those pins without risking dropping at least one. And when you do, the consequences can be significant.

There is a solution. There is always something that you can do to make a difference. You just need some new ideas – good advice and good planning. This book is about helping you to become more financially independent of your business. I hope you find it useful.

'Annual income twenty pounds, annual expenditure nineteen [pounds] nineteen [shillings] and six [pence], result happiness. Annual income twenty pounds, annual expenditure twenty pounds ought and six, result misery.'

~ Charles Dickens, *David Copperfield*

The Big Picture

1

The 6 Pillars of Financial Success

Small business owners are passionate – they love to talk about their business. Those in retail, for example, often can't walk past a store without looking at the layout, range, new ideas, etc. They love what they do. But they are mostly focused in the business – getting the day-to-day work done. If you are a retailer, it's about the store, the stock. If you sell tiles, for example, you can no doubt talk all day about the detail on tiles, glazing, who makes the best tiles, trends, prices, and so on, and never tire of it.

There is more to becoming successful, however, than merely focusing *in* the business.

Working *on* the business (managing it to stay profitable) and working *beyond* the business (balancing work and family and creating a personal financial plan) complete the trinity of business success. Aligning these three facets under a single program of six steps, six pillars, enables you to achieve success and financial security, which is what this book is about.

Your business may be doing well even if you, the owner, come off second best, without any real financial reward at the end of the day. However, true financial success and security, both for you and your business, lies in you becoming financially and operationally independent of your business.

CADTRE is my acronym for these 6 steps, your 6 Pillars of Financial Success. I believe in these principles so implicitly that I named my business CADTRE Consulting – everything I do for my clients focuses on helping them to achieve this holistic level of success and personal freedom, and is what I urge you to consider when focusing on your own situation.

CADTRE stands for:

Cash flow management

Asset management

Debt management

Tax management

Risk management

Estate and succession plan/exit strategy management

Over time, this integrated approach and the resulting actions can make an enormous difference. With this, you can achieve:

- Improved business and personal cash flow
- The means for a better lifestyle
- Control of your exposure to business and personal risks
- Potentially higher net worth
- Better balance between business, lifestyle, and investment assets
- A stronger and more valuable business
- Effective systems and processes to manage both business and personal finances

The following chart shows how you, as a business owner, can build your business and wealth and become financially independent of your business before you retire. The split in net assets (asset value after subtracting debts/liabilities) is what CADTRE enables you to reap from your business in order to set yourself up for life.

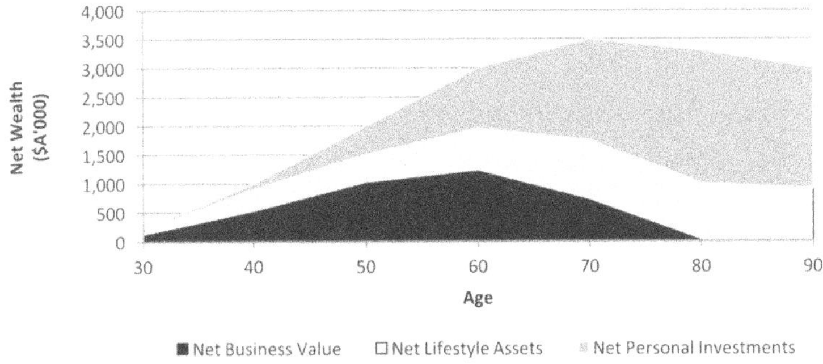

Typically, lifestyle assets (your home, etc.) and your business represent the bulk of your wealth, offset by the money you owe: your mortgage, personal obligations, and business debt. However, as your business grows, say, between the ages of 35 and 50, harvesting some of the cash flow to build up quality investments outside your business can better enable you to become financially independent of your business by, say, age 60. That is what you want to do, what we will do together using the 6 Pillars, to achieve real financial security for you, without your having to depend on the success of the business to stay afloat.

In the chart above, by age 60 to 80, you progressively sell out of the business. If, for some reason, the business is not saleable or the value of the business cannot be realised, it is still possible by age 60 for you to retire and be reasonably comfortable because your investment assets are now on par with the value of your home, giving you a reasonable investment base upon which to retire. Clearly, a key objective would be for you to sell your business, and do so at a good price. However, as illustrated above, by having used the 6 Pillars to establish your financial security, your financial future would not be dependent on you being able to do so. That's what I mean when I say your goal, as a small business owner, should be to ultimately become financially independent of your business.

When delving into these areas in greater depth – cash flow, assets (including investments), debt, tax, risk/reward, and estate and succession planning – they can become very technical and specialised, which is when a financial advisor or other expert can make a huge difference.

We will focus instead on the big picture as the best way to start. You need the big picture to ensure you cover all your issues, not just one or two, in order to achieve the necessary balance that financial success requires. The custom detail work can – and should – follow later. For now, we need to start by giving you a foundation so you have something to build upon.

Once you are ready for more detail or need to understand these areas in more depth, that is the time to talk to your accountant, lawyer, or qualified financial advisor.

How to Get Started

As a small business owner, you face many of the basic financial issues and challenges of larger businesses, but without the same level of resources, while also grappling with all the challenges and financial issues that we, as individuals, face. In order to be truly successful, you need to develop and work on both your business and personal financial plans. Why? Because they share a common denominator – YOU.

While it sounds logical, a surprising number of business owners fail to do this. As a result, tensions rise and clashes occur concerning what the business is doing versus what the owner and family want to do. More often than not, these clashes arise from poor cash flow management and an inability to balance personal and business demands sufficiently. But it doesn't have to be this way. I am going to show you how you can change this.

Like most good things and successful outcomes, it involves:
- Knowledge and understanding
- Planning and setting priorities
- Hard work – making necessary changes and getting things done

For example, if you are overly integral to your business to where it cannot function without you, and your family's welfare is tied up heavily in the business's profit level, what happens to the business and your family if something happens to you? Even a temporary disability could prove financially devastating for everyone involved without a plan in place.

Think of the 6 Pillars of Financial Success as progressive points on your journey to financial freedom, the interim steps you will take to reach your destination. However, before you can map out the journey you want to take, you need to first decide on your destination. *You need to establish your goals.*

Setting Goals

Goals, both business and personal, are your destinations. And a clear plan is a roadmap designed to take you there the most efficient way possible. Without a roadmap, it's easy to get lost. As American baseball player Yogi Berra famously said, 'If you don't know where you are going, you'll end up someplace else'.

And that might not be the place you want to be.

Setting goals, and tracking to these goals, puts you in the driving seat. Having a concrete idea of where it is you want to go yields a higher chance of success than just hoping for the best. It makes it far easier to balance your business life against your personal life. And it helps you immediately spot which goals might conflict or create obstacles that block you reaching other goals so you can resolve them and keep moving forward.

For example, if you find yourself with a surplus, is your first instinct to spend the money on a deposit for a new machine for the business? Or would you rather take that overseas vacation you've been yearning for but keep putting off? Either one could be the right answer for you. The new machine may be just what you need to grow your business, if it represents a good return on investment, but if equipment finance is not your preferred option, there is a conflict. Having a plan in place helps you to establish what your priorities are – and to honour them.

With established goals, your business can head in the direction you are comfortable with whilst it supports or complements the direction you want your life outside your business to head. The financial and time commitments you make to your business can be weighed up against your personal goals and priorities. The trade-off and compromises you make can be weighed up to better inform the decisions you make so that you and your family are comfortable with them.

This is different from the 'boiling frog' situation, where the heat is turned up so slowly at first that you don't realise you're in hot water until it's too late to escape. You want to be comfortable with what you have to do from the start, winning both in your business and at home.

To accomplish this, you need to stand back and assess where you want to go – to see the proverbial forest rather than be blinded by the trees right in front of you. Being able to stand back and see the whole picture can be very powerful, and is one of the big benefits of planning. People who take the time to make plans tend to make more of an effort to work towards them. Often, they serve as a guided missile. You now hit your targets more reliably.

Some people avoid setting goals, as they do not want to fall short and be disappointed. They have a fear of failure that gets in the way of succeeding. Yes, not getting there is disappointing, sometimes even painful. The trick is to see it not as a failure but as an experiment or learning opportunity. When you fail to get to where you want to go, you have learned that the route you chose wasn't the right one. Maybe the road was closed. Maybe the bridge you thought you would find does not exist. You just need to adjust – to re-program that internal GPS – and move forward again. Standing still never gets you anywhere but where you are right now.

The result of falling short often depends on the degree of risk you take. Set business and personal goals and make sure they align instead of being counter to one another, as in the example above of choosing between buying a new machine or taking a trip. Effective goals have clarity, are quantifiable, and are assigned a timeline as to when you would like to achieve the goal. Providing this clarity is not always easy; however, being clear and precise about what you want to accomplish increases your chances of achieving your goal.

An all-or-nothing approach is too high a risk in most situations. Smaller, more thoughtful steps increase your chance of accomplishing what you set out to do. This way, having a goal is likely to put you in a better position than standing still or relying on luck.

You make your own luck when you set realistic and achievable goals that are yours – ones that resonate with you and reflect where you want to ultimately be – and when you make a plan, setting out the necessary steps you need to take to reach them. It puts you in the driving seat and empowers you, both in your business and your personal life. It is not enough to say, 'I want the business to be profitable', or 'I want to make a million dollars by the time I am 40'.

I'm not saying that making a million dollars by the time you're 40 is not achievable. But the idea is to set precise, realistic, reachable goals, such as specific sales targets within a period of time. Only with concrete goals can you set achievable steps to reach those goals.

You might consider setting yourself (and your team, if appropriate) 'stretch targets'. For example, if you were a competitive runner, you might set a goal that would force you to stretch beyond what you have already proven you are capable of, such as improving your endurance by achieving a faster speed or covering a greater distance.

A stretch target for a salesperson might be to increase overall sales by a slightly higher percentage or dollar amount than ever before, to increase sales by a specific degree with existing clients, or upping the number of new customers you sign each month. Stretch targets challenge you so you do not shift into autopilot and simply cruise along. For them to work, getting close to, while still falling short of, your target needs to be seen as a good thing, not that you have failed. They drive you to make tangible progress and improve your position.

Never underestimate the power of having a plan. You are halfway there when you have a good plan.

One of my clients was acquired by a US stock-exchange-listed company. Part of the deal included an 'earn-out', which meant earning further shares based on performance, and part of the deal was a companywide computer system upgrade.

This client's original business did not generally prepare a business plan or annual budget. Part of the acquisition included doing this, reporting to the US parent company, and more – all tasks that were new and demanding. It was a big adjustment to get to the new planning and reporting level.

For this business, achieving budget – hitting the numbers – was vital, making realistic targets a better choice than stretch targets.

A number of years after the acquisition, the improvement in the business's results was outstanding, with growth in revenue generally in the 10–15% range.

To achieve this transformation, the following key changes were made:

1. Implementing the new computer system
2. Improving the team – hiring some new staff and clarifying staff roles so all bases were covered, including the new planning and reporting work
3. Closing the books and accurate numbers at each month's end
4. Preparing a realistic business plan and budget with input from the management team, and making sure they were committed to both
5. Implementing the changes and tracking daily/weekly/monthly to the plan

Making a plan energises you. It builds confidence as well as excitement, and sets a direction for the business to head in and targets to aim at. It does not, on its own, guarantee success, but it is the next step. Having this map, and sharing it with all the team members, ensures that all the team members pull the business in the same direction instead of working at cross-purposes. And that puts you one step closer to success – success as YOU define it.

Establishing Your Mission, Vision and Values

Start by defining your business's mission, vision, and values. Be specific. List them and post them where you (and your team) can see them.

Your mission is what your business sets out to do. For example, 'to sell artisan baked goods' may be factual, but your mission should be a bit more specific, such as 'Our goal is to sell quality, value-priced artisan baked goods citywide (or online, or whatever your target region may be)'.

Your vision is where you see your business in, say, five years. Using the artisan baked goods example, your vision might look like this: 'To become the premier online source for artisan baked goods throughout Australia'.

Your values are essentially what you stand for, the principles you abide by in doing business, such as to treat your customers fairly and honestly, to ship orders within a certain timeframe/provide prompt service, and/or to offer an unrestricted, no-questions-asked return policy – whatever principles guide how you do business belong here, in your list of values.

From this point, you can begin to build a plan, which will also explore whether your business goals are financially feasible long term.

Key Points

- CADTRE represents the 6 Pillars of Financial Success: cash flow, assets, debt, taxes, risk, and estate plan/exit strategy.

- To head in the right direction and succeed, you need to know your precise destination – what it is you specifically want to accomplish.

- Set goals, both business and personal, and track your incremental progress.

- Create your business's Mission, Vision, and Values – what you stand for and what your business's focus is – and post it where you and your employees can see them every day. Live by them.

2

Top Challenges for Small Businesses

No Money + No Help + No Time = No Way Forward

Small business face a wealth of challenges, but the primary obstacles to success are generally:

Too-tight cash flow – Cash flow management must be a top priority. Often, the focus drifts *away* from first bringing in money (collections) and spending within one's means.

Insufficient help/support – It's not enough to make do with what you have rather than actively seek what you need. That kind of approach is not sustainable and will eventually undermine the business. You need to identify the right resources to address gaps and weaknesses.

Too hands-on – An over-reliance on the owner creates unnecessary excess financial and personal risk. The owner becomes a captive of the business and can never escape.

Too-Tight Cash Flow
Assuming for now that the success of your business, defined by its cash flow, is the primary generator of the cash that funds your

Peter Gialouris

lifestyle, either as drawings or a salary; if you fail to manage your business's cash flow effectively, that can severely diminish the amount of money available to you to draw as income.

Conversely, if you fail to manage your personal cash flow effectively, and personal expenses exceed your income to the point where you must draw more money out of the business to stay afloat than you'd budgeted, those excess withdrawals can inhibit the growth and success of your business.

The point is that these two cash flow areas should not be viewed as independent. They are, instead, interdependent. As a business owner, you need to be on top of both your business cash flow AND your personal cash flow to succeed. Depending on your business, cash flow is driven by sales, collections, operating expenses, and capital expenditure. For many days, weeks, and months, cash flow can be negative, where you find yourself (hopefully temporarily) in the red.

Cash flow problems are generally the result of spending more than you have. Where businesses are concerned, overspending may be combined with insufficient customer collections.

You need to make business collections a key priority, almost as high a priority as making the sale. Your personal costs – living expenses, especially discretionary expenses – need to be reined in, if you're having difficulties. Do this and you are a long way towards controlling and solving the problem of too-tight cash flow. If you don't, it becomes a battle between keeping your business and personal financial selves afloat and you're left treading water, your head barely – if at all – above the surface. Learning how to swim is how you avoid drowning.

Insufficient Help/Support

Small business is not a solo sport. Despite being in the driving seat, you need a good team working with you in order to be successful. Your team may consist of family members, one or more partners, employees, or perhaps simply one or two advisors—a lawyer, or an accountant. As your team is smaller in size than those of larger businesses, *each and every team member counts.* This is true no matter how minor any role may seem.

As a small business owner, you have likely trained yourself to make do with what you have, rather than actively seek what you need. Whilst cost may be a reason, it often has more to do with a lack of planning. By identifying the gaps and resource issues that exist in your situation, you can methodically tackle them in order to make them cost effective over the long term.

For example, it may be difficult to attract staff; alternatively, you may not require permanent staff, but merely assistance during peak times and seasons. You might want to consider contract providers or outsourcing part of the work instead.

Yes, it is possible that you and/or your key staff can buckle down and keep assuming more and more responsibility, as tasks increase. Most small business owners argue in favour of this, claiming, 'This way it gets done, and done right', but such an approach exerts enormous strain. Whilst this may suffice right now, it is not typically sustainable and can risk undermining your business.

What if your business continues to grow? Can you and any staff continue to take on ever-increasing responsibility in order to keep up? It is hard to keep working like this without the risk that you will burn out. When you are too tired to continue treading water, that's when you go under.

The time you spend to plan ahead and work on putting in place a more sustainable solution is an investment that can pay off handsomely. Remember, the idea here is to break free of captivity, not to enslave yourself further, no matter how passionate you are about your work and your business. You want your work to add to your life, not to become your life.

Too Hands-On

As a business owner, it is inevitable that you are the heart and soul of your business, the key driver of its success. Successful business owners know that while they are pivotal to their business's success, it is critical to extricate themselves from every aspect of the day-to-day operations by building a competent support system, a team that ensures that the business can function competently without the full attention of any one individual.

If this isn't done, and done properly, you can find yourself tied up in the business – a captive – both in how it operates and how you finance those operations. What you do not want is to have a business that restricts what you can do personally. If your home secures some of the business finance, it might restrict you from buying an investment property, or partaking in other forms of borrowing and investing. Not only that, if the business fails, your family's home is now at risk.

If you are tied up physically in your business, you may feel the need to be involved in every day-to-day facet of the business for it to work. While this might make you feel you play an important role, it is a recipe for disaster. Many books on climbing the corporate ladder stress how important it is not to make yourself indispensable to the point where you won't be promoted because no one else can do your job as well as you do. Small business owners face that same risk, but it carries an even greater cost: if anything happens to you, even for a short while, the business will likely fall apart. Obviously, that is not what you want, or at least not what you should want. Part of the solution is getting the right help – solving the No Help portion of the equation.

If you are too tied up financially in the business, you need to address the financial goals and issues you have that lie *beyond* the business. The objective is to reduce your business and financial risk (which will also reduce your stress levels). This is achieved by limiting to a minimum the amount of personal security and guarantees you provide for the business. Personal insurance, superannuation, asset protection, and estate planning are other options that lessen your personal financial reliance on the success of your business.

The 'too tied up' position can be very confronting. Like the story about the little Dutch boy with his finger plugging the leak in the dyke, you can't leave the business, not for a single minute, without risking your safety, your livelihood. Some small business owners can't leave the shop even to go to the toilet. Does that describe you? Are you in hock, financially tied up? Is your home on the line?

Freeing yourself up as the owner, far from making you irrelevant, can make the business more fun for you, and the passion that got you into business in the first place returns.

Add to these three challenges an additional challenge:

Focusing beyond the business – To succeed, business owners must balance the success of the business with their personal financial position.

While it's understandable that the majority of your energy has been focused on what's going on *in* the business, a holistic approach is necessary. Focusing *on* your business means focusing on the issues to improve the management and profitability of the business, while focusing *beyond* it means managing your personal financial position. You must allocate some time to each of these three.

Instead of, say, working 100% in the daily operations of the business, scale your time spent back to 85% and put maybe 10% more to working *on* the business and the remaining 5% on *beyond* the business.

How? You need to offload that added 15%, the more routine work, to another good pair of hands.

By doing this, the **No Money + No Help + No Time = No Way Forward** equation can be addressed. By ensuring that your business plan and actions and your personal plan and actions complement each other and work in tandem, a clear way forward appears and synergy is created.

There are plenty of books that focus on improving a small business by working *in* the business more efficiently and effectively, using tools like computerisation or more targeted marketing. Books that focus *on* their business zero in on how to be a better manager. And there are books that exclusively address the area *beyond* the business: the personal financial plan, including insurance, superannuation, investment strategy, business exit strategy, and more.

As a small business owner, however, you need to focus on all three of these, to varying degrees, with the starting point being to improve how you focus *in* the business.

**Money Sorted + the Right Resources + Time/Freedom
= The Way Forward**

Key Points

- Small businesses are most often challenged by too-tight cash flow, inadequate support, and the owner (and the owner's personal assets) being too integral to the success of the business.

- It's not enough to focus *on* the business; you must also focus on life and your future *beyond* the business.

Your Business, Your Plan

Goals
- To boost your bottom line and resulting cash flow
- To make your business more profitable and valuable
- To improve your personal financial position and reduce your exposure to the business

Learn how to
- Assemble and perform a comprehensive financial results review, including net worth calculation
- Establish and maintain a schedule for regular reviews so you always know where you stand
- Devise a business plan, including overview, SWOT (strengths, weaknesses, opportunities, threats) analysis, strategy setting, cost-benefit analyses, cash flow reports, budgets, and forecasts to streamline your review process
- Devise a personal financial plan to launch you on the path to financial freedom and security
- Align your business and personal plans so they work together instead of against each other

3

The Results Review

Before you can make a plan for the future, you need to know where you stand right now. This is where a results review comes in.

A results review is, by definition, immediate and reactive – *tactical*. The development of your Business and Personal Plans, by contrast, are longer term and proactive – *strategic*. Both are part of working *on* your business.

A results review reveals the strengths and weaknesses in these three areas:

1. Cash flow
2. Resources
3. Alignment issues

In practical terms, what does this mean?

A results review can be very structured, or it can focus more on identifying and dealing with exceptions. Proactive approaches are typically thought out in advance, before any disaster might strike. It's a bit like attending a fire prevention class, or stocking and maintaining fire extinguishers and sprinkler systems in case of emergency – think of it as a form of insurance.

Reactive approaches are undertaken when or after disaster strikes. It's putting out the fire after it has caused damage. As the old saying goes: *A stitch in time saves nine.* No one wants a major setback or loss when simple preventative measures can be put in place – prevention is better than cure. Disputed invoices are a good example, relatively

Peter Gialouris

easy to resolve if tackled right away, whereas 6–12 months later, it becomes potentially much harder to resolve and results in significant delays in getting paid.

It means using and reviewing the financial information that you have. Once a results review is undertaken, it is helpful to consult someone, such as your accountant, who can 'read' the numbers and work through them with you. A regular review and analysis of the numbers provides very useful metrics and financial information – see it as a scoreboard for your business.

You should review your business's cash flow and revenue ideally on a daily basis but at least every week. That means looking at the weekly/daily sales, the amount banked, amount spent, and the bank reconciliation. Every week you should review the accounts receivable, accounts payable, gross profit generated, net profit, and sketch out the following week's cash flow forecast.

Your profit & loss statement and balance sheet should be reviewed monthly, at minimum. Review the status of your working capital, existing debt, and compare your current situation against the previous year's and the forecasted budget, often referred to as benchmarking.

Let's take a quick look at the kind of strengths and weaknesses a results review can uncover.

Scenario

Lesley and Tom Cann run a business together selling niche medical equipment. Tom is 40 years old, Lesley, 39, and they have two children, ages six and eight. Their business is called TLC Stat Medical Supplies, registered as a proprietary company in Australia, and is based in Sydney, New South Wales. They maintain a staff of 15 employees.

Even if this example seems worlds away from the kind of business you run, the premise is the same for every small business, whether it be a distributor, supplier, service provider or independent contractor. The focus here is on *how you do it*, not *what you do*.

This first worksheet provides a snapshot of the financial situation of Tom and Lesley, both personally and professionally.

	$ Business	$ Personal	$ TOTAL
Profit and Loss			
Revenue	5,000,000		5,000,000
Cost of sales	(3,500,000)		(3,500,000)
Total Gross Profit	1,500,000		1,500,000
Operating Expenses	(1,500,000)		(1,500,000)
Net Profit Before Tax	**0**		**0**
Balance Sheet/Net Worth			
Fixed Assets	200,000		200,000
Bank Overdraft	(300,000)		(300,000)
Equipment Finance	(100,000)		(100,000)
Accounts Receivable	1,000,000 (600,000 over 30 days)		1,000,000
Inventory	500,000 (200,000 slow-moving)		500,000
Net GST Payable	(20,000)		(20,000)
Accounts Payable	(710,000)		(710,000)
Other creditors & Accruals	(75,000)		(75,000)
Provisions	(100,000)		(100,000)
Bank		5,000	5,000
Home		1,000,000	1,000,000
Mortgage		(500,000)	(500,000)
Lifestyle Assets		200,000	200,000
Investments		0	0
Super		300,000	300,000
Net Assets	**$395,000**	**$1,005,000**	**$1,400,000**

This worksheet has flagged several weaknesses:

1. In terms of customer collections, relative to sales, too much is tied up in accounts receivable – $600,000 is more than 30 days and past due. Following up overdue accounts, resolving any invoice disputes that might be holding up payments, and clarifying customer credit terms and credit limits would bring in most of the $600,000 overdue. It would also reduce the level of overdue balances going forward, strengthening their cash position and possibly eliminating the existing bank overdraft.

2. A large portion of the inventory is slow moving, whether the result of the need to keep demo equipment or spare parts, ordering errors, cancelled orders, etc. Some of this inventory may be needed to support the business. A plan to discount and move ordering errors, or demo equipment no longer required, for example, could improve cash flow significantly. Internal systems and procedures could be improved to address mistakes made, resulting in a reduction in required inventory, permanently improving the business's cash position.

3. Business profitability is too low. An analysis of pricing, foreign currency management, handling and charging of freight on-costs, and operating costs in general, could improve gross profit to 5–10% of sales – possibly $250,000–500,000 net profit before tax.

Now let's look at how things might improve should these weaknesses be addressed. Insurance cover has been increased to eliminate gaps (and will be reviewed/updated again in one year) and Tom and Lesley assigned one member of their staff to serve as a sales representative in Melbourne, expanding their customer base/location and adding $200,000 in new revenue. In addition, after addressing the weaknesses outlined above, you can see how the changes made increased their bottom line, either by adding value or decreasing debt. Net profit after tax increased by $210,000 and net assets increased by nearly 50%. In addition, considerable goodwill was created by these improvements, also adding to the overall value of the business.

	$ Before	$ Change	$ After
Profit and Loss			
Revenue	5,000,000	200,000	5,200,000
Less Cost of sales	(3,500,000)		(3,500,000)
Gross Profit	1,500,000	200,000	1,700,000
Operating Expenses	(1,500,000)	100,000	(1,400,000)
Net Profit before tax	0	300,000	300,000
Tax Expense	0	(90,000)	(90,000)
Net Profit After Tax	**0**	**210,000**	**210,000**
Balance Sheet			
Fixed Assets	200,000		200,000
Bank (Overdraft)	(300,000)	400,000	100,000
Equipment Finance	(100,000)		(100,000)
Accounts Receivable	1,000,000	(300,000)	700,000
Inventory	500,000	(100,000)	400,000
Net GST Payable	(20,000)		(20,000)
Accounts Payable	(710,000)	210,000	(500,000)
Other Creditors & Accruals	(75,000)		(75,000)
Provisions	(100,000)		(100,000)
Net Assets	**$395,000**	**$210,000**	**$605,000**

The benefit, both immediate and long term, of making these kinds of financial reviews a regular discipline, cannot be overstated. You are the one who benefits. And if you don't do it, you are not the only one who is going to get hurt—your family and your staff are going to feel the pain as well.

Cash Flow

Cash flow is the financial lifeblood of any business. No matter how good the product or service you provide, or how strong the customer base is, without sufficient cash flow a business will eventually fail. This cash flow needs to be harnessed, both to run the business and to pay you, the owner, an affordable and commercial level of drawings or salary.

The same can be said on a personal level. You need to manage your personal cash flow to support the best life possible within your means.

The art of doing this is to establish clear goals and priorities. And you need to prioritise your spending and track how much is going where.

It's not how much you earn but what you do with it.

Often the key is simply to keep tabs on your spending and focus on your priorities. If you don't, there will never be enough money. Money is a precious resource, like water. Even where water is abundant, it is irresponsible to waste it. You never know when its source might dry up – when there might be a drought.

You need to respect your cash flow, manage it carefully, and always keep an amount in reserve for when money is tight, business is tough, and/or an emergency strikes. A number of years ago I helped out a high-powered lawyer with a large legal firm. He had a life partner, no children, and earned more than half a million dollars a year. He came to me because despite his substantial income, he could not make ends meet. He had run up a six-figure debt, including a number of credit cards. His lifestyle involved entertaining on a lavish scale – his liquor bill alone was equal to the annual household budget for some Australian families. His problem? Because he knew his income was generous, he assumed it was enough and made no real attempt to track where the money went.

Once we sat down and figured out where it was all going, and he could see it in black and white in front of him, he was able to take concrete steps to reduce over spending and not just eradicate his debt and make ends meet but regularly save money. We consolidated his credit card debt into a less costly loan with a lower interest rate and established a repayment plan. He went from being an ostrich with his head in the sand to keeping an eagle eye on what came in and went out. Instead of feeling burdened by this, he was astonished at the freedom, the feeling of flight, it gave him.

The value of performing regular reviews of your business results and cash flow really hit home for a client of mine. Unfortunately, disaster struck, in the form of a devastating computer crash, during which their back-up system also failed, the business had no access to any accurate, up-to-date numbers. They were sailing through a fog, towards the rocks.

To recover, it was necessary to sit down and manually reprocess 18 months of transactions. That is when the wisdom of my recommendation really hit home. We started to review the numbers weekly, and hold a monthly management meeting. Only then did it become apparent that if the business did not change course, it would eventually fail. The mistake the owner had made was in thinking that because he was an integral part of operations, he knew everything that was going on. We made the necessary changes and the business today is thriving.

TIP: It's a smart idea to regularly ensure that your back-up system is functioning correctly. If you use a cloud-based back-up system, consider what it might mean for your business if you found yourself unable to access the internet/cloud in an emergency and plan accordingly.

A disciplined regular review system will almost certainly save you considerable headaches down the road. This is what I recommend to my clients:

Business Results and Cash Flow Review Checklist

	Daily	Weekly	Monthly	Quarterly
Accurate Numbers (Accounts)	Ideal	Preferred	Minimum	
Bank & Cash Flow	Preferred	Minimum		
Sales & Gross Profit		Preferred	Minimum	
Collections & Accounts Receivable	Preferred	Minimum		
Payments & Accounts Payable	Preferred	Minimum		
Payroll		As required	As required	
Profit		Preferred	Minimum	
Balance Sheet		Preferred	Minimum	
Tracking to Budget/ Business Plan			Preferred	Minimum

Key Points

- Review cash flow and revenue daily, or at least weekly.

- Review accounts receivable, accounts payable, and gross/net profits weekly.

- Review profit & loss statement, balance sheet, working capital, and debt, and benchmark numbers against previous year and any forecast on a monthly basis.

4

Your Business Plan

No business can function well long term without a plan in place. The same can be said of our personal lives. Without a vision for the future, and an idea or map as to how to achieve what it is we want, we risk drifting off course, sometimes irrevocably.

A good example of this is the development of a new product. Without a detailed plan, the best idea may never realise its potential, or you might run out of funds and be forced to sell the idea/innovation before its true value can be captured.

For example, a small Australian company developed a machine that was world class, completely ahead of global competition. The enthusiasm for the idea and what it represented was so great that management forged ahead, confident that the value of the idea itself would carry them through. They never got around to sitting down, carefully researching what was involved in its development, and making a plan so that they would be going in with their eyes wide open, ready for what this ground-breaking idea entailed.

Developing the prototype, followed by a production model that could be sold worldwide, proved to be very expensive and time consuming. The machine needed to be easy to operate, safe to use, and meet the various Australian and foreign regulations and quality standards before being marketed. It had cost five times more than initially expected and put enormous pressure on the business. But that wasn't the end of it. Once it was developed and ready for sale, selling the machine overseas and protecting the knowhow required even deeper pockets.

If the company had first detailed a plan to develop the prototype and production model and sell the machine, and performed a financial analysis, they would have had a far better idea of what lay ahead and could have considerably improved upon the success of the project.

Setting financial parameters regarding the capital investment required by the project and reassessing the situation in a measured way would have helped. Testing the overseas market, assessing the risk of it being copied, and having a plan to recoup the investment through early sales and profits or protect their IP, the intellectual property, was also needed. In hindsight, a joint venture with a larger company in the industry or selling the IP might have proved the better course.

Socrates observed, 'The unexamined life is not worth living'. Taking the time to execute a plan is to examine how your business works, to ensure not just that it is worthy of your time but that it will indeed provide for you a life worth living – that it will satisfy you and help you achieve what in life will truly make you happy.

Starting with an extensive, highly detailed plan can present a huge hurdle for some, especially if you are already struggling to find time to incorporate the recommendations I've made. Don't panic. Even a small amount of thinking and planning, and some direction, is better than no direction and no plan at all. A good place to start is with the short form plan, and build from there.

Your business plan can be concise, no more than one or two pages, as long as it is fully thought through, feasible, and tested – whether the numbers stack up.

Appendix A contains a blank standard short form financial plan worksheet that you can reproduce and use to sketch out your business plan using the guidelines below.

Be sure to include financial targets and metrics for the next three years to have as your goalposts. Be realistic and choose achievable targets. Choose calculated risks versus unnecessarily big risks, and outline steps to cover any downside.

As we walk through the development of a business plan step by step, we will use the example from the previous chapter, TLC Stat Medical Supplies, to illustrate how this can be done. The earlier results review showed the various weaknesses the business was unaware of and what can happen when you shine a light on them and take action to improve the situation. The next step for TLC, following a results review, would be to set out a business plan to move from short-term actions to a longer-term strategic plan, and address longer-term issues and opportunities.

Once the Sydney operation was running well, I would recommend a plan to examine and act on:

1. The possible expansion of the business into other Australian states and how this could be implemented, as expansion can significantly boost profits and the value of the business. Options include flying into other states from Sydney, hiring a sales representative in one or more other states, or setting up branch offices.

2. Developing a well-considered plan for staff and resources to ensure there is depth and the business works as an effective and robust team. The long-term solution is not to have Tom and Lesley assume more responsibility. Identify and address business gaps and team performance issues.

3. Examining whether it might be better to own the business premises rather than lease, particularly if Tom and Lesley's

home is not securing the premises. This can potentially enhance the value of the business and reduce the risk on their family home, if the commercial property can guarantee the mortgage instead. Options include offering to buy the current location, buying elsewhere and relocating the business, or whether more attractive leasing opportunities exist elsewhere.

4. Increasing business insurance cover by engaging an insurance broker to analyse the needs of the business, identify any gaps, and ensure adequate cover of property, staff, and owner and business interruption risks.

Once the shorter-term business issues are addressed through the results and cash flow review process, and a business plan is devised and implemented to address the longer-term business building and planning issues, with an annual review, the business can become a very robust and powerful engine. That can help Tom and Lesley build their personal wealth and financial security, knowing they are in a much stronger and proactive position to deal with issues that arise and take advantage of opportunities.

Step One – Business Overview

List the business's Mission, Vision, and Values.

Let's say that TLC's mission is: 'To be a reliable supplier of quality medical equipment and supplies to medical centres and private hospitals'.

TLC's vision might be: 'To become the premier supplier of medical equipment and supplies throughout Australia in the next five years and create positive brand recognition within the industry'.

TLC's values might include:
- To deal with our customers promptly, fairly, and honestly.
- To ship all orders in less than 30 days.

- To respond to queries and complaints within ten days.
- To support each community in which we maintain an office by donating medical supplies to local schools and charitable organisations.
- To run our business in an environmentally responsible way – to be 'green'.

If you have not already done so, take a moment now to think about your business. What is its mission? What is your vision for its future? Jot your ideas down and formulate a one-sentence mission that captures these, and note it either in the form in Appendix A or somewhere where you can see it regularly.

Now, give some thought to what your values are – what do you and your business stand for? What is important to you? What values do you have that might benefit your customers if they knew? Be honest with yourself when writing these down. Don't be tempted to include items that might sound impressive but are not truly important to you. You want to limit this list to what you believe in, so that you can live these values through your business.

Now, put together a list of your business's goals and objectives. Be specific and use measures where possible – dates, sizes, percentages, etc. Here are some possible examples for TLC's business.

- Expand the Sydney-based business into Melbourne and Brisbane
- Maintain the current exclusive Australian product distribution rights for all of its existing foreign manufacturers (list each company and country)
- Secure the Australian distribution rights to (list quality foreign manufacturers currently not sourced)
- Increase sales by 10% on previous year
- Generate new online sales of $500,000

Step Two – Create a SWOT Analysis

List every strength, weakness, opportunity, and potential threat that your business possesses or faces. Be comprehensive – really think this through. Use the TLC example below to get started.

Sample SWOT Analysis	
Strengths	**Weaknesses**
• Top brands • Reputation for quality • Excellent customer service	• Lack of skilled staff in key areas • Owners too hands-on; need to delegate • Poor cash flow position • Business risks not adequately covered • No succession plan
Opportunities	**Threats**
• Potential expansion into online sales • New offices in nearby Victoria and Queensland could expand customer base	• New competition from innovative, high-quality, and less expensive medical products developed by Chinese, Japanese, and Korean manufacturers

Step Three – Actions and Plans/Strategies

The strategies you list here should capitalise on the strengths and opportunities and address the weaknesses and threats you have identified after performing the SWOT analysis above. Include all options you might consider and any cost-benefit analysis (see below). Should you expand interstate? Buy that new machine? Branch out into a new business area?

Include financial targets, guideposts and metrics for the next three years. These are your goalposts.

Peter Gialouris

Make sure your plan is realistic and has a reasonable chance of achieving these targets. It's okay to be ambitious – part of doing this work is to calculate what is and isn't feasible. Just be careful when considering taking big risks and ensure you cover your downside. Avoid all-or-nothing gambles. Take calculated risks you can comfortably afford.

For TLC, a list of strategies might include:

Sales & Marketing	– Hire new salesperson in Melbourne
	– Promote online sales
Operations	– Invest in new systems and technology to enhance productivity
Staff	– Hire new staff
	– Skills development training plan for current team
Financial	– Funding plan for next three years and address business risks, including a disaster recovery plan and more robust business insurance cover
Systems and IT	– New system to integrate sales, operations, and finance
	– New website

Step Four – Cost-Benefit Analysis

If you are not familiar with how to perform a cost-benefit analysis, it is a bit like jotting down the pros and cons before deciding on a course of action. Ultimately, you want to determine the anticipated cost of something and calculate whether the benefit of doing/ purchasing something outweighs the costs, and if so, by how much.

In this instance, you identify a consideration, such as a capital expenditure – investing in a relatively expensive piece of machinery – and jot down all the pros and cons in terms of whether it will benefit you/your business. An expense like this might save you in terms of labour, time, cost savings, or all three.

List all those who will benefit from such an acquisition: you (the owner), partners, staff, the business itself, customers/clients, suppliers. Computerising your business may cost you in terms of initial time spent but serve to make recordkeeping far more efficient and less time consuming long term. Software might eliminate the need for a bookkeeper, or reduce the hours they need to spend on a regular basis.

Consider the effects it might have on those who are not directly involved, such as how freeing up your time might mean you can spend more time interacting with clients and customers. This includes family members, if the ripple effect of such an acquisition frees you sufficiently to spend more time with them, or frees up cash flow to where you can provide money for education, investments, better living environment, a vacation or vacation home, activities for the kids, or a hobby, for example.

Choose a relevant period, whether it's months or years, and list all the benefits and associated costs.

Admittedly, this is an overly simplified version of what a cost-benefit analysis entails, but you get the idea. An accountant can help you with this if you are unsure how to accurately project and calculate costs and benefits. It is a particularly important exercise when contemplating making major changes, such as a large capital expenditure, particularly one that might require financing.

Sometimes a cost-benefit analysis can be initiated by simply polling your customers. A hairdressing business planned an extensive fit-out of their premises and then ran the idea past their customers. To their surprise, the majority of the customers said they were content with the way things were. What they really wanted was better quality coffee.

The expensive fit-out was abandoned and a good coffee machine purchased instead. The end result? Significantly less expense and happier customers.

Step Five – Organisation Chart, Current and Planned

Your business's organisation chart includes everyone on your team – all employees, partners/co-owners, volunteers – and their respective roles. Note whether all key functions are covered, or whether there are any staffing gaps, and any key areas for improvement or restructuring, to build and develop the team. (If you don't identify and resolve these, the problems end up in the too-hard basket for the owner – you!)

For TLC, the plan might be to hire a new salesperson in Melbourne in Year 1 and another in Brisbane in Year 2 or 3.

Step Six – Current Annual Budget and Years 2 and 3 Projections

This includes your profit & loss, balance sheet, and cash flow. A monthly break-up of your Year 1 budget helps to track and assess your progress. Feel free to use your own profit & loss and balance sheet formats if you prefer, or consult your accountant – this is merely one suggested format.

Profit & Loss

	Initial [1]	Current [2]	Year 1/ Budget	Year 2	Year 3
Sales – NSW	5,000,000	5,200,000	5,720,000	6,292,000	6,921,000
Sales – VIC			500,000	550,000	605,000
Online Sales			500,000	650,000	845,000
Sales – QLD				500,000	550,000
Total Sales	5,000,000	5,200,000	6,720,000	7,992,000	8,921,000
Cost of Sales	(3,500,000)	(3,500,000)	(4,435,000)	(5,195,000)	(5,799,000)
Gross Profit	1,500,000	1,700,000	2,285,000	2,797,000	3,122,000
Gross Profit %	30%	33%	34%	35%	35%
Overheads					
Staff	(1,000,000)	(1,000,000)	(1,170,000)	(1,358,000)	(1,498,000)
Rent	(120,000)	(120,000)	(180,000)	(240,000)	(250,000)
Other Expenses	(380,000)	(280,000)	(350,000)	(400,000)	(450,000)
Total Operating Expenses	(1,500,000)	(1,400,000)	(1,700,000)	(1,998,000)	(2,198,000)
Net Profit	0	300,000	585,000	799,000	924,000
Tax	0	(90,000)	(176,000)	(240,000)	(277,000)
Net Profit After Tax	0	210,000	409,000	559,000	647,000
Capital Expenditure		(25,000)	(25,000)	(25,000)	(25,000)
Asset Disposals					
Other Major Items (Specify)					
Dividends paid to shareholders			(20,000)	(30,000)	(40,000)

Balance Sheet & Cash Flow Projection

	Initial [3]	Current [4]	Year 1/ Budget	Year 2	Year 3 [5]
Bank Balance (Overdraft)	(300,000)	100,000	100,000	518,000	1,012,000
Trade Debtors	1,000,000	700,000	817,000	899,000	989,000
Inventory	500,000	400,000	739,000	866,000	966,000
GST* Receivable	10,000	10,000	14,000	15,000	18,000

Other Current Assets

	Initial [3]	Current [4]	Year 1/ Budget	Year 2	Year 3 [5]
Total Current Assets	1,210,000	1,210,000	1,670,000	2,298,000	2,985,000
Fixed Assets	200,000	200,000	215,000	230,000	245,000
Total Assets	1,410,000	1,410,000	1,885,000	2,528,000	3,230,000
GST* Payable	(30,000)	(30,000)	(48,000)	(53,000)	(58,000)
Trade Creditors	(710,000)	(500,000)	(554,000)	(649,000)	(725,000)
Other Creditors	(25,000)	(25,000)	(26,000)	(28,000)	(29,000)
Accruals	(50,000)	(50,000)	(53,000)	(55,000)	(58,000)
Provisions	(100,000)	(100,000)	(110,000)	(120,000)	(130,000)

Other Current Liabilities

	Initial [3]	Current [4]	Year 1/ Budget	Year 2	Year 3 [5]
Total Current Liabilities	(915,000)	(705,000)	(791,000)	(905,000)	(1,000,000)
Loans	(100,000)	(100,000)	(100,000)	(100,000)	(100,000)
Total Non-Current Liabilities	(100,000)	(100,000)	(100,000)	(100,000)	(100,000)
Total Liabilities	(1,015,000)	(805,000)	(891,000)	(1,005,000)	(1,100,000)
Net Assets	395,000	605,000	994,000	1,523,000	2,130,000
Issued Capital	100,000	100,000	100,000	100,000	100,000
Retained Earnings B/F	295,000	295,000	505,000	894,000	1,423,000
Current Year Profits (Losses)	0	210,000	409,000	559,000	647,000
Dividends paid	0	0	(20,000)	(30,000)	(40,000)
Total Equity	395,000	605,000	994,000	1,523,000	2,130,000

Notes from *Profit & Loss* and *Balance Sheets*

1, 3   Before changes from results review were implemented.
2, 4   After changes from results review were implemented; some period of time will inevitably elapse between the time you first review your results, identify and implement the necessary changes that can be made immediately (or within a short period of time) and when the business plan is updated/finalised. It shows the value of the improvements made and the importance of tracking your progress.
5   This Plan should result in very strong cash flow being generated and funds being made available to invest further in the business, buy the business premises or invest further in investment assets outside the business, like clearing the mortgage and maximising contributions into super. The big challenge is to stay on track and achieve the plan then harvest the gains made. More actions can be taken and the plan updated as the results are achieved.
GST*   Goods and Services Tax: overall GST is less that 10% of purchases and sales due to deferred GST on imported items and GST-free sales of some medical supplies.

Cash Flow Report

For cash flow reports, there are two common formats. One is a gross receipts and payments format. Not all accounting systems provide this information easily; however, if your business works on a cash accounting basis, you may prefer this format.

The second format is the one used below, and is the one more commonly used by accountants. It starts with net profit and adjusts it for the movement in the balance sheet to show you your cash flow on a net movement basis. This suits businesses that work on an accrual accounting basis. Accrual accounting provides more accurate and complete profit & loss and balance sheet figures.

Important considerations include whether you need a cash flow injection or expect the business to self-fund and generate sufficient cash flow. You want to identify the expected cash flow over the coming three years, especially Year 1, in order to analyse whether or not you might need to inject money to fund your plan.

Performing a regular cash flow analysis encourages you to be proactive, anticipate problems and issues, and take advantage of opportunities. Use it to:

- Set goals and develop strategies for the next three years
- Prepare financial targets to ensure the numbers stack up and you stay on track
- Track to your plan, and review/update it annually

TLC Stat Medical Supplies Cash Flow Report

	Current*	Year 1 Budget	Year 2 Projection	Year 3 Projection
Opening bank balance	(300,000)	100,000	100,000	518,000
Net Profit after tax	210,000	409,000	559,000	647,000
+ Depreciation		10,000	10,000	10,000
- Capital Expenditure		(25,000)	(25,000)	(25,000)
+ Disposals				
± Decrease in Current Assets	400,000	(460,000)	(210,000)	(193,000)
± Increase in Current Liabilities	(210,000)	86,000	114,000	95,000
- Dividends		(20,000)	(30,000)	(40,000)
± Increase in loans		0	0	0
Net cash flow	400,000	0	418,000	494,000
Closing bank balance	100,000	100,000	518,000	1,012,000

*After changes from results review were implemented.

The best way to deal with business cash flow issues is through a regular review of collections, outgoings, and profitability, either by you or a financial professional. This usually involves a daily, weekly, and/or monthly financial management process.

A short form Business Action Plan and annual update can address any lack of appropriate resources and you, the owner, being too tied up in the business.

As we have discussed, this Plan should result in a strong cash flow being generated and opportunities to invest further in, or outside, the business. External investments may include clearing a mortgage or in investment assets within super or outside super.

The big challenge is achieving this cashflow improvement. At this stage, the business plan would be updated to allow for the redeployment of this surplus cash. Either to reinvest within the business or pay a bonus or dividend to Tom and Lesley and factor this into their personal financial plan. This is where the synergy and alignment of the business and personal financial plans, and the potential for conflict, arises. I stress here that your realistic plan to improve the business and achieve results needs to come first – and that's the hard work.

Annual Review

An annual review and update of your financial plans will address strategic gaps, enable you to revise old targets as needed and set new ones, and implement actions to take the business forward.

Is your business going in the right direction? What business changes are foreseeable that you need to plan for? Is your succession plan and exit strategy still current? These and many more issues should be evaluated regularly – annually at minimum – to ensure that you remain current instead of falling behind.

Changes can occur internally, such as a shift in your goals and priorities and your personal circumstances. External factors, those outside of your control, also change over time and it is critical to stay on top of them. External factors, particularly those that impact your business, include such items as government regulations and tax structures, your business's sector/industry/marketplace, changes in technology, demographics, and potential threats and opportunities.

What's Next?

Now that you have detailed your business results and cash flow review process and completed the short form business plan, it's time to do the same for you, personally. Once you have both of these completed, they can be assessed against each other to ensure they align instead of conflicting in some way.

Key Points

- Keep your initial business plan simple – you can build from there.

- Choose realistic targets and avoid overly risky strategies/goals.

- When writing down your Mission, Vision, and Values, think hard about what is most important to you. The list doesn't have to be long; it just has to resonate with you.

- When devising your SWOT analysis and strategies, ask those who know you and your business well for input. Consult an advisor or mentor once you have noted everything you can think of – an expert opinion can highlight items that might never occur to you.

- A cost-benefit analysis is a valuable tool to help define the pros and cons, costs and profits, from any decision or capital investment.

- An overall annual review enables you to identify and address gaps in a timelier manner and map your progress.

5

Your Personal Financial Plan

Think of your personal financial plan as a personal business plan, designed to uncover any and all weaknesses and issues that need to be addressed that might prevent you from achieving your personal financial goals.

For example, if your business plan is to borrow money, which entails increasing the level of personal security you provide as the owner of your business, that might mean using your family home as financing collateral or making personal guarantees. Your personal financial plan's goal, however, might be to reduce the level of security you must provide and your personal exposure to business risk. In that situation, your business and personal financial plans conflict.

Many financial plans recommend maximising contributions into superannuation. However, if sufficient cash flow is not available within the business, or the business needs those funds in another capacity, the super strategy might be abandoned, a circumstance that might benefit the business but not you, the owner. That is why integrating the two is important.

The integrated business and personal financial plan we will explore now, and the underlying review process on your business and personal cash flows, addresses the problems that most small business owners face.

Your personal financial plan deals with:

Cash Flow – To better manage your personal cash flow and ensure you are living within your means and what your business can afford and fund

Resources – To identify and address any gaps and weakness and seek any resources you need, such as expert financial advice if you wish to create a self-managed super fund

Owner Freedom – To reduce the extent to which you are tied up financially and at risk to your business

Alignment Issues – To identify any existing or potential conflicts between your business and personal financial plans in order to facilitate their integration and alignment

Using our example of TLC Stat Medical Supplies, owners Tom and Lesley Cann have completed the business review and planning and it has already put them in a stronger position. However, some initial strategies could make a difference, such as:

- Create an emergency cash reserve fund of $50,000
- Free up the family home from securing the business and accelerate mortgage repayments using the increased business cash flow
- Build up the superannuation fund to provide for retirement, benefit from tax concessions, and increase asset protection; analyse possible benefits of having a self-managed super fund own the business's real estate
- Ensure insurance and estate plans provide adequate protection (income protection, trauma cover, possibly increase their existing life and disability cover, and consider tax effectiveness of insurance options within super as well as outside super)

and that these complement their business insurance and succession plans.

The personal financial planning process is similar to the business plan process. Use the same short form supplied in Appendix A that we used in the previous chapter but tailor it now to your personal affairs.

Be sure to take a moment to consider the Mission, Vision, and Values sections. These don't apply just to business. Your mission might be to provide financial security for your family while spending quality time with them, outside the business. Your vision for the future could be to retire by a certain age – where do you want to see yourself in, say, five years? And your values are those most important to you in terms of how you choose to live your life.

Remember, the focus of this plan is on your financial position *outside* of your business, and your financial independence and security. The end result will be your lifestyle and how comfortable you and your family will be.

Putting this all down in black and white gives you six steps to follow, which are expanded on over the following pages:

Step 1: Information on your current position and goals
Step 2: An assessment of weaknesses, issues, and gaps
Step 3: The opportunity to investigate options and strategies, including obtaining professional advice
Step 4: Establish current and projected annual budgets
Step 5: An action plan to implement specific changes
Step 6: The motivation to regularly schedule ongoing reviews to stay on track

Step One

Information

Personal Goals – Your personal goals naturally drive your personal financial plan. As discussed in the section on business goal setting, you need to decide on your destination before you can map out a route. After all, if your dream is to retire at age 50, it is not going to happen if you don't calculate how much money you will need to do so and save accordingly.

Think long and hard about what it is you really want. Much has been said in recent years about the importance of setting SMART goals – specific, measurable, attainable, realistic, and timely – and justifiably so. It is not enough to say your goal is to be successful. You need to define concretely what success means to you. A more specific goal might be to earn your first million dollars by age 35, for example (specific and measurable). Can it feasibly be done – is it attainable? Is it realistic, based on your current age and cash flow, and can it be done within the necessary timeframe? Using this approach will help you set priorities and balance or align conflicting objectives, both within your personal life and in how these goals impact your business.

An alternative goal might be to work less; to reduce the number of hours you work. How many hours specifically do you wish to reduce your weekly commitment to? Can it be done? How? What alterations or adjustments would you need to make in terms of staff, perhaps taking on a partner, so that your reduced involvement in the business doesn't negatively impact business cash flow and prevent you from achieving this goal? How quickly would you like to accomplish this? Is that feasible? If not, how long would it take you to accomplish this?

Rather than seeing this as a chore, see it as a step towards freedom. It shines a light on what you want to do so that you can eliminate unrealistic goals (and the frustration your inability to achieve them would inevitably bring) and allow you to focus on what you can do, concretely, to improve your quality of life and overall sense of satisfaction. Once you outline what you want, you can begin to list the steps you need to take to get you there.

Calculate Your Net Worth – Your net worth is the sum of all your assets, from which you subtract all your liabilities (debts). So, if you were to liquidate everything you own and pay off all your debts, how much would you be left with?

Bear in mind that, depending on your level of personal and/or business debt, your current net worth could be a negative number. If it is, don't panic. More often than not, that's the case for younger individuals, those just out of university or starting out in a new endeavour. Your current net worth is simply information that is important to know as you set out your plan, a number that establishes your starting point.

Gather all your related information and keep it in a single folder that you will update at least once a year. Once you have all the information handy, start calculating. List individually your largest assets first, such as your home and any other real estate, vehicles (including boats, ownership in a private plane, etc.), and the current value of your business (less any liens/loans), business-owned vehicles, and machinery. Use current market values and avoid the temptation to exaggerate the value of any item. Don't deduct any mortgage or loan values just yet. Calculate each asset's value as if it were free and clear.

Use the Net Worth Calculation form provided as part of Appendix A at the back of the book to list all your liquid assets – savings, investment, and retirement accounts. Finish by adding in any personal items of notable value, such as artwork, jewellery, or valuable stamp or coin collections.

Together, they represent your total available assets.

Now, list your most significant debts and liabilities, such as the mortgage on your home, business financing, and car/boat/plane loans, and their current outstanding balances.

Next, include any other personal debts, such as loans and credit card debt. Add these all together to see what your total liabilities are.

Now, subtract your total liabilities from your total assets. This is your personal net worth. Again, don't be alarmed if this is a negative number. The goal here is to establish a starting point from where you will track your progress annually (at minimum). That way you can see relatively quickly whether you're falling behind or getting stronger.

For Tom and Lesley, their net worth statement would look like this:

Net Worth Statement	
Assets	**Initial**
Personal / Lifestyle Assets	
Residential Home	1,000,000
House Contents	200,000
Collectibles	
Jewellery	
Car 1	
Car 2	
Caravan / Boat	
Holiday Home	
Total Lifestyle Assets	1,200,000
Investments / Savings	
Savings / Cash Management Trust	5,000
Term Deposits / Bonds	
Rental Property	
Managed Funds	

Assets	Initial[*]
Shares	
Life Insurance Cash Value	
Net Business Equity	395,000
Superannuation Assets	300,000
Super contributions	
Other	
Total Investment Assets	700,000
Total Assets	**1,900,000**
Liabilities	
Home Loan	(500,000)
Loan Offset Account	0
Additional Loan repayments	
Investment Loan	
Car Loan	
Personal Loan	
Credit card	
Student Loan	
Other Loan	
Total Liabilities	**(500,000)**
Net Worth (Assets Minus Liabilities)	1,400,000

[*] Before any changes from results review are implemented.

Now, let's calculate existing cash flow – your cash flow is your personal income less your personal living and other expenses. It is similar to your business's profit & loss statement – income, less expenses.

Tom and Lesley's cash flow statement would look like this:

	Initial*
Income	
Salary	150,000
Business Income/Dividends	
Investment Income	
Other Income	
Income Tax Payable	(32,000)
Medicare Levy Payable	(3,000)
Net Income	115,000
Expenses	
Lifestyle Expenses	(80,000)
Home Loan	(30,000)
Personal Loan or Line of Credit	
Investment Loan	
Investment Expenses	
Other Expenses	
Total Expenses	(110,000)
Annual Estimated Cash Flow	5,000

*Before any changes from results review are implemented.

Step Two

Assess weaknesses, issues, and gaps

See this as your personal SWOT (strengths, weaknesses, opportunities, threats) Analysis. List every strength, weakness, opportunity, and potential threat you can think of to your current financial position. Be comprehensive – really think this through.

Tom and Lesley's would reflect their need to:

- Establish cash reserve/rainy-day fund
- Reduce home loan
- Build up super fund
- Ensure adequate insurance and protection is in place

Step Three

Options and strategies

The strategies you list here should capitalise on the strengths and opportunities and address the weaknesses and threats you have identified after performing the SWOT analysis above. Include all options you might consider, along with any appropriate cost-benefit analysis.

A list of strategies for Tom and Lesley would include:

1. Set up and begin funding a personal cash reserve
2. Improve personal cash flow position
3. Increase home loan repayments
4. Put in place more robust personal insurance cover (one that protects them and not just the bank)

Step Four

Current Annual Budget and Years 2 & 3 Projections

A monthly break-up of your Year 1 budget helps to track and assess your progress. Feel free to use your own format, if you prefer, or consult your Financial Advisor/Planner – this is merely one suggested format.

Begin first by entering only your current income, expenses, and net worth from your earlier cash flow calculation. (Figures for Years 2 and 3 will be added later.)

	Current	**Year 1**	**+ / -**	**Year 2**	**+ / -**	**Year 3**	**+ / -**
Total Income after tax							
Total Expenses							
Net Cash Flow							
Net Worth							

Tom and Lesley's figures would look like this:

	Current	**Year 1**	**+ / -**	**Year 2**	**+ / -**	**Year 3**	**+ / -**
Total Income after tax	115,000						
Total Expenses	110,000						
Net Cash Flow	5,000						
Net Worth	1,400,000						

A more detailed plan for Tom and Lesley, completed for Years 1, 2, and 3, might look like this:

	Initial [1]	Change	Current [2]	Year 1	Year 2	Year 3
Income						
Salary	150,000	50,000	200,000	200,000	210,000	221,000
Business Income/ Dividends				20,000	30,000	40,000
Investment Income						

	Initial [1]	Change	Current [2]	Year 1	Year 2	Year 3
Other Income						
Income Tax Payable	(32,000)	(18,000)	(50,000)	(57,000)	(65,000)	(73,000)
Medicare Levy Payable	(3,000)	(1,000)	(4,000)	(4,000)	(5,000)	(5,000)
Dividend Franking Credit				9,000	13,000	17,000
Net Income	115,000	31,000	146,000	168,000	183,000	200,000

Expenses

	Initial [1]	Change	Current [2]	Year 1	Year 2	Year 3
Lifestyle Expenses	(80,000)		(80,000)	(80,000)	(84,000)	(88,000)
Home Loan	(30,000)		(30,000)	(30,000)	(30,000)	(30,000)
Personal Loan or Line of Credit						
Investment Loan						
Investment Expenses						
Other Expenses						
Total Expenses	(110,000)	0	(110,000)	(110,000)	(114,000)	(118,000)
Annual Estimated Cash Flow	5,000	31,000	36,000	58,000	69,000	82,000

Notes

1 Before changes from results review were implemented.
2 After changes from results review were implemented; again, this documents the improvements made initially, after the first results review has been performed to identify gaps and weaknesses.

Net Worth Statement

Assets	Initial	Change	Current	Year 1	Year 2	Year 3
Personal / Lifestyle Assets						
Residential Home	1,000,000		1,000,000	1,000,000	1,050,000	1,103,00
House Contents [1]	200,000		200,000	200,000	210,000	221,00
Collectibles						
Jewellery						
Car 1 [2]						
Car 2 [2]						
Caravan / Boat						
Holiday Home						
Total Lifestyle Assets	1,200,000	0	1,200,000	1,200,000	1,260,000	1,324,00
Investments / Savings						
Savings / Cash Management Trust	5,000		5,000	5,000	5,000	5,00
Term Deposits / Bonds						
Rental Property						
Managed Funds						
Shares						
Life Insurance Cash Value						
Net Business Equity	395,000	210,000	605,000	994,000	1,523,000	2,130,00
Superannuation Assets	300,000		300,000	334,000	371,000	410,00
Super contributions [3]						
Other						
Total Investment Assets	700,000	210,000	910,000	1,333,000	1,899,000	2,545,00
Total Assets	1,900,000	210,000	2,110,000	2,533,000	3,159,000	3,869,00

Assets	Initial	Change	Current	Year 1	Year 2	Year 3
Liabilities						
Home Loan	(500,000)		(500,000)	(470,000)	(440,000)	(410,000)
Loan Offset Account [4]	0	31,000	36,000	50,000	50,000	50,000
Additional Loan repayments				44,000	113,000	195,000
Investment Loan						
Car Loan						
Personal Loan						
Credit card						
Student Loan						
Other Loan						
Total Liabilities	(500,000)	36,000	(464,000)	(376,000)	(277,000)	(165,000)
Net Worth (Assets minus Liabilities)	1,400,000	246,000	1,646,000	2,157,000	2,882,000	3,704,000

Notes

1 House contents are depreciating assets; any increase is the result of having added new items of value.

2 In this particular example, no value is assessed to vehicles because they are owned by the business and, as such, are calculated as part of the value of the business's assets and liabilities.

3 In this plan, paying off the home loan has been assigned priority over boosting super fund contributions; surplus funds have gone towards additional home loan repayments. Once the home loan is cleared, increasing super contributions and other investments will be the next priority. (This is why having surplus cash flow creates opportunities and allows Tom and Lesley to continue building and setting themselves up for the future.)

4 The loan offset acts as the emergency cash reserve until the home mortgage is repaid, providing accessible funds and reducing home loan interest, and is tax effective. (It also provides a high interest rate on available funds as the mortgage rate is higher than their at call cash management account rate.) The starting balance of $36,000 is made up of the initial cashflow surplus of $5,000 and the additional $31,000 shown above.

Step Five

Action Plan

Task	Person Responsible	Due Date
Establish cash reserve – loan offset account	Tom & Lesley	Within 3 months
Personal insurance review	Tom, Lesley, and specialist insurance advisor	Review within 3 months; new cover implemented within 6 months
Increase loan repayments	Tom & Lesley	Within 12 months
Review super	Tom & Lesley	Within 12 months
Review estate plan (Wills, Enduring Power of Attorney etc.)	Tom, Lesley and Estate Planning Specialist	Within 3 months, then every 3 years or as required
Review personal financial plan and business plan progress	Tom, Lesley and relevant advisors (e.g., accountant and financial planner)	At least annually

Step Six

Ongoing review

This review is like the business results and cash flow review completed in the previous chapter for your business. A personal financial review at least every 12 months is the minimum you should do. Depending on how active your financial affairs are, e.g., if you have a direct share portfolio or a self-managed super fund (SMSF), a more frequent review may be required. Including a specific advisor, such as your financial planner, is very useful when undertaking this process. They can help you analyse how you are tracking, what changes you should make, and implement some of the changes.

This is what I generally recommend to my clients:

Personal Financial Plan Review Checklist

	Monthly	Quarterly	Annual
Bank Accounts	Minimum		
Cash Flow	Minimum		
Investments			Minimum
Credit Cards & Loans		Minimum	
Tax			Minimum
Insurance			Minimum
Estate Plan			As required, or every 3 years

Align Your Business and Personal Plans

Start by scrutinising both plans, side by side, and identify any potential conflicts. Which take priority? Note each one and make a list of possible solutions in order to better align them.

It is critical that the priorities you set, and the choices and trade-offs you are willing to make, are realistic and feasible. Calculate your projections for how any changes you intend to make will appear in Years 2 and 3 in the chart above. Those are your goal numbers. When you do your next comparison, in a month, in six months, in a year – whatever you choose – the idea is to compare how you are doing in Year 1 versus your Year 1 projections. If you are doing even better than projected, adjust your projections for the coming years, as appropriate.

In the above example, the improvement in the business and the cash flow position will create opportunities allowing both the business to be expanded further and/or to harvest some of these gains – take a trip, upgrade your home, or invest in assets outside the business such as in your super fund or an investment property.

But the gains need to be made. When that's done many exciting options will be opened up, and there is no right answer on what to do with the money. In our example, that depends on what Tom and Lesley wish to do and these desires should be factored into their personal financial plan.

My suggestion – and a key reason for writing this book – is that I believe you need to allow the business to expand and to harvest some of these gains. That is why you need to align your *business plan* and your *personal financial plan*. If you don't do this, opportunities may be missed and conflicts and regrets may arise. This dual view can also create a powerful synergy between and commitment to both plans – a feeling that the business is working and working *for you* and you are getting the rewards for the effort, sacrifices and risk being taken.

Fruits of Your Labours

After reviewing your business results and crafting both a business plan and personal financial plan:

- Your business and personal goals are or will soon be aligned. (You are now on your way to working *in, on,* and *beyond* your business.)
- You are on the front foot when it comes to managing your business and personal cash flows – you know exactly where you stand financially.
- You can identify and tap the necessary resources you need to get where you want to go.
- You are taking steps to avoid being held hostage by your business and to become financially independent of it.

Key Points

- Managing your personal cash flow more efficiently enables you to spot gaps and weaknesses that can be addressed before they get out of hand. Reviewing it regularly also prevents unwelcome surprises.

- Setting personal goals is as important as setting business goals – remember, the real goal is to ensure the business builds financial security for you personally, to enable you to support a comfortable lifestyle outside/independent of the business.

- Don't panic if your current net worth is a low or even a negative number. Information is power. Once you identify where the weaknesses are, you can set about addressing them and driving your net worth up.

- Budgets aren't restrictive – they're actually liberating, but most people don't realise that. When you develop the confidence that comes from knowing how much money is going in versus going out, you'll not only sleep better but look forward to the future with greater anticipation.

- Decisions to redirect cash flow to areas like retirement savings will be more positively impactful if you sit down with your advisor first and ensure your choices carry the least risk and the greatest benefits for your individual situation.

- Aligning your business and personal plans enables them to work together towards the same goal – your financial security.

Applying CADTRE: Your 6 Pillars for Financial Success

C – Cash flow (Harnessing)

A – Assets (Building and preserving)

D – Debt (Controlling)

T – Tax (Minimising)

R – Risk (Protecting)

E – Estate & Succession Plans (Tailoring)

Goals

- To apply all 6 Pillars to both your business and personal affairs, and ensure the two align instead of conflict
- Identify any gaps and weaknesses
- Establish and adhere to a regular review of financials

Learn how to

- Harness your cash flow so it works harder for you
- Build and preserve your assets, the foundation of your financial security
- Control debt to manageable proportions
- Minimise tax liabilities and obligations, putting more money in your pocket
- Identify and protect against various forms of risk and identify gaps where protection needs to be introduced or bolstered
- Establish an effective succession plan, both for short-term emergencies and your eventual exit from the business
- Put in place an estate plan to protect your dependants in the event anything happens to you while you are still operating your business

6

C: Harnessing Cash Flow

Competent cash flow management is the recipe to build wealth, like a soufflé rising in the oven under your watchful eye.

Consistently spending more than you earn is a recipe for disaster. Consistently spending *less* than you earn, on the other hand, is a recipe for success.

I once had a client whose accounts staff found every excuse not to contact customers to collect delinquent payments. They would gladly pay the bills but not ring and follow up overdue accounts. I was able to resolve it, fortunately. Sometimes, you may not be aware that the person handling this is putting it off. Perhaps other things seem to always come up that justify taking priority. Some owners abdicate rather than delegate this responsibility. Delegating is fine. Abdicating is playing with fire. And, as the owner, ultimately it will be you who gets burned.

Business Cash Flow

As a small business owner, you rely on your business to generate sufficient cash flow to fund your lifestyle. To do this, it needs to be well managed – with what I call a military focus, meaning well disciplined. Managing cash flow deserves your attention as much as generating sales and revenue, because it is not enough to have lots of money coming in if the money going out regularly exceeds that amount.

Sales and revenue are the lifeblood of any business – they are a core reason for being in business. That involves getting paid. Accounts receivable (AR), or debtors and collections, is vital.

In too many small businesses, collections are an afterthought, what someone reluctantly does only if they have time or when cash flow is critical. But collections deserves a position far above crisis management. If your accounting person (which might be you) pays the bills first and refuses to chase money unless forced to, things are going to get tight, and fast. This is not difficult to remedy. You simply need to reorientate your perception.

Collections can be a strength of your business, a part of developing good working relationships with your customers in ways that ensure you get paid on time. The way to do this is to establish and maintain clear, agreed upon credit terms and limits, and regular follow-up. Make the follow-up process a positive experience by making it one that:

1. Acts as a reminder for customers (sometimes invoices do inadvertently get overlooked)
2. Catches missing invoices or dispute issues so you can resolve them more quickly
3. Can tell you when a customer is in difficulty and not likely to pay, allowing you to take action as early as possible to minimise any potential loss
4. Can create increased rapport with your customers to stimulate collections

People in business understand that their suppliers need to be paid. The timing of payment – accounts payable (AP), or creditors and outgoings – needs to be managed as well, *before* the money is spent, i.e., at the purchasing stage. Capital expenditure items are important too. There needs to be a connection between the payment terms with your suppliers and the credit terms your customers have in order to manage and minimise that funding gap.

This is a day-to-day process in most businesses. The ones that are good at it and are proactive, especially with collections, are on top of their cash flow. The ones that are not on top of their cash flow are forced to operate in a reactive way, on the back foot all the time. Cash flow issues cause stress, can put customers offside, and end up wasting time and money. No business can afford to do that.

Regular – I suggest daily – follow-up by a key person or team within the business and a weekly meeting with you as the owner on the cash flow position, forecast, etc., can make cash flow a strength of the business.

Being on top of your cash flow or experiencing a turnaround feels very empowering and provides a tremendous boost for the business. I experienced this turnaround not only in the above example but in many businesses, including a high-value, leading-edge medical technology company, and a graphic design business. In all cases, they needed someone to drive the process and work with the owner.

You need to delegate as much of the follow-up work as you can, and have a robust system, but don't abdicate here. Whether you deal with it yourself or have others deal with it for you, you need to keep enough of a handle on it to ensure the team is on top of it. At a minimum, that means keeping an on eye on the bank account and the weekly cash flow forecast. Let's look at how to do this.

How to Approach Collections

Chipping away at overdue accounts in a targeted way is easier than letting them build up into a mountain to climb. Perhaps for you it means making two or three priority follow-up calls or emails a day, rather than 10–15 calls or emails in one hit.

Types of overdue accounts

Overdue debtors generally fall into one of the following three categories:

1. **Customers who need a gentle reminder** – These customers usually pay up with one, two, or three follow-up phone calls or emails. Think of it as checking as to whether the customer is happy and what else might need to be done to ensure the customer is satisfied.

2. **Invoice issues or disputes** – These customers typically have a question regarding the amount invoiced, have in fact already paid, or have never received the invoice. Once the issue is addressed, the collection can be sorted out and you will have preserved your relationship with another good customer.

3. **Bad debts** – These debtors are bad news, deliberately delinquent, and unless you are firm and proactive, they will not pay. This category is hard work. You need to identify these debtors early and not extend them any further credit.

Thankfully, the debtors in category 3 usually represent a very small percentage of unresolved collections. Most customers fall within the first two categories – they need either a reminder or an invoice issue to be resolved. *These debtors require a customer service attitude and approach.* When you strive to build a rapport or friendly relationship with the customer, collections usually improve over time.

The best way to ensure prompt collections is to establish a good system *before* making a sale. Here are six basic steps to create an effective collections system:

1. **Establish Credit Terms** – Ensure the credit terms and credit limit for each customer is clear and has been agreed to up front, so there is no confusion as to whether invoices are due in, say, 7, 14, 30, or 60 days, and that they know there is a maximum allowable credit up to whatever dollar amount is viable for your business.

    If a customer uses purchase orders to approve purchases, or a central payment system (often located overseas), it is important to clarify this up front. Ensure you are given a copy of the purchase order and that your invoice either matches it or that any variations have been approved. Don't get tangled up in these issues by thinking the local person you are dealing with will always go into bat, or cut corners, for you. Make sure your paperwork complies with their system.

2. **Perform regular review and follow-up** – Review and flag overdue accounts at the very least on a weekly basis – daily, for better results. *Make it a part of your normal work activities.* Follow up on customers with the largest outstanding balances first to maximise the impact payments will have on your cash flow.

3. **Obtain contact person and commitment data** – It sounds like hard work, but a number of friendly follow-up calls can greatly improve your control over collections. Make sure the customer has the outstanding invoice(s), agree with the amount(s), is happy, etc.

    - Phone or email the customer to determine when they will pay
    - Keep good records: maintain a log of the name and contact details of the key person, when contacted, and the payment date promised
    - Ask the person you are dealing with to commit to paying the account by a certain date, even if it is later than

you would like, or just a partial payment to start. If the customer is having difficulty making payments, getting a number of small amounts to eventually clear the account can be a mutually acceptable alternative approach

- Where you are dealing with a central payment system, whether domestic or overseas, include your customer's local contact in the follow-up process so they can help you navigate their payment system

  If payment is not received by the date promised, follow up and get a new commitment to a payment date. Usually, one to three follow-up calls will get the account paid, either in full or via a number of partial payments. Friendly follow-up calls can typically get at least 50% of overdue accounts from categories 1 and 2 to pay without a lot of fuss or bother. And approaching the call from a customer service perspective can make touching base with your customer a pleasant experience instead of an unpleasant one

4. **Respond to issues and disputes promptly** – If the customer has not paid due to an invoice dispute, record the name and contact details of the person you are dealing with and work with them to resolve the difference. They may be stalling, but chances are they want their records to be correct and will work with you to bring their records in line with yours.

   Perhaps a customer has already paid but you have no record of receiving the amount. In the case of an electronic payment (EFT), contact the bank regarding the status. If the payment was made by cheque, they may need to cancel and reissue it. If they say they never received an invoice, reissue one immediately. And then follow up.

   If the customer uses a purchase order or central payment system, make sure the necessary paperwork is in place and that there are no reasons or excuses to delay payment. Don't assume it will all magically be okay. Be proactive and work with your local contact to cover all bases *before* you deliver the goods or service. If you trip up here, it can take months to get paid. And if you wait until you have already delivered the goods or service, you are in weaker position, with little leverage.

5. **Continue to work the system** - Continue to follow up on overdue accounts until invoice issues are resolved and the account is collected (or formal collection proceedings need to commence).

6. **Make it a team effort** – If you have an accounts person to do follow-up, ensure they escalate problem accounts, meaning they request assistance from sales or senior management, or you, the owner, when necessary to facilitate the collection process. The sale is not complete and doing business with the customer is at risk if the matter is not resolved and the outstanding invoice is uncollected.

What can happen?

Collections can become a strength of your business and build a stronger relationship between you and your customers. This will improve your cash flow and result in more customers paying you within the agreed upon credit terms.

Remember to:

✓ Keep in touch with your customers – a friendly reminder
✓ Ensure invoice amounts and credit terms are clear and agreed upon
✓ Resolve any issues promptly
✓ Identify non-payers early and take action

✓ Make collections a customer-friendly part of your business, like sales and service

It's not a sale until you get paid, so complete the sale by addressing collections on a daily basis.

Personal Cash Flow

Cash flow management is equally vital at the personal level. Some owners use their business as an ATM machine, withdrawing funds as needed for personal reasons. This can cause havoc.

Ultimately, the most responsible practice is for the owner to take a set level of drawings or salary that is commercial and affordable and work within that. Where there are good years and the business can afford to pay a bonus or a dividend, then taking extra funds out can work in those circumstances. Otherwise, stick to a set affordable amount and let the business run unimpeded.

It is vital to grasp what your essential living expenses (food, clothing, mortgage, utilities, etc.) and discretionary expenses (overseas travel, entertainment, hobbies, and so on) come to, and to have a simple, maintainable system to keep track of it all.

Some people set a household budget and stick to it. Others struggle to do this or choose to bury their heads in the sand. The cash flow management system I recommend to my clients uses your main bank account as a fuel gauge. It is up to you to keep an eye on the gauge.

If you start to fall below the level you have set, you take action. If you build up funds above this level, you can invest, re-deploy, or allocate those funds however you wish.

The beauty of this system is that it is a proven, workable way to manage your money when you retire and begin to live off your investments. It provides you with the tools to manage your money and your cash flow, and not only make it last but harness it in order to spend it wisely on what matters to you. Otherwise, it can all too easily slip through your fingers.

The goal is to consistently spend less than you earn. An excellent savings target is to put aside at least 10% of your income for emergencies and retirement savings. If you genuinely cannot manage 10%, do yourself a favour and make it as close to 10% as you possibly can. Think of your available income as being 90% of your total income. If you can spend even less, even better.

Dipping below the cash reserve level indicates that you are spending more than the annual level you have set. Building up funds above the reserve level indicates that you are spending less and have funds available for reinvestment.

A Workable Cash Flow Management System

I recommend that you set up a fairly simple system, one that is not daunting to maintain, so that it can easily become a weekly, even daily habit, and one that, when you start seeing those savings add up, becomes enjoyable, even exciting.

The first step is to assess your total salary/drawings. Start with your monthly income. Now, calculate what 90% of that number is. That is the number you will use to gauge your cash flow levels.

Now, write down your fixed and relatively fixed personal monthly expenses, such as rent/mortgage, insurance payments, utilities, groceries, petrol consumption, childcare or education, and debt repayment. Go through your chequebook and credit card statements to ensure you don't overlook anything.

Now, write down your discretionary expenditures, such as entertainment, vacations, charitable donations, dining out, subscriptions, gym memberships or other fitness costs, etc. Don't worry about being too detailed – just stick with the fairly consistent expenses for now. Remember, you want to include what's significant but still keep it simple enough to stay on top of it.

During this exercise, make sure you split your regular daily living expenses, e.g. food, petrol etc, and your less regular, less frequent living expenses, e.g. rent or mortgage, your monthly and quarterly bills etc.

Now, total up all your regular expenditures and see how much of your monthly income (the 90% number) that total represents. Are you spending less than you make? If so, well done! Are you spending more than you make? Then it's time to take a harder look at where your money is going in order to control your expenditures. Make it your goal to make your expenditures total no more than 90% of your income, and ideally less, so that you have a further cushion for unanticipated or impulse expenses that don't qualify as true emergency expenses. Think of it as giving yourself an annual 10% bonus, one that you can invest so it grows even further.

The next step, if you haven't done this already, is to open a dedicated bank account for your cash reserve, the account you will use for emergency and non-regularly scheduled expenses. This is NOT the bank account you use on a regular basis for living and recreational expenses. This reserve must be liquid, secure, have online access/visibility, and earn a competitive interest rate in order to keep this fund working for you. Now, set it up so that you pay ALL of your income into this account.

Once you have this set up, you transfer the amount you need to fund your regular daily living costs into your regular daily banking account. This daily account must feature an ATM and online access to give you visibility at any given moment. It is from this daily account that you will pay your regular daily living expenses. Use your cash reserve to pay the less frequent living expenses, such as your rent, mortgage and monthly and quarterly bills.

As the regular daily living expenses should be fairly consistent and the minor part of your total living expenses, your cash reserve account will become your 'fuel gauge' and cash flow scoreboard, and an easy way to assess your cash flow position at any time.

Do NOT use your cash reserve account for unforeseen discretionary expenses such as an impulse vacation or dining splurges. Only do this when you are ahead – when you have built up the funds and are above the cash reserve level you have set for your rainy-day fund and buffer.

Monitor your daily and cash reserve accounts no less than once a week. When your cash reserve balance exceeds the buffer amount you have set (i.e. how much you would need to live on for six months or longer if you would prefer a higher amount should anything happen to halt your salary/drawing income), invest those surplus funds in a recommended investment vehicle.

Warning Sign

Don't get caught dipping below your cash reserve level. If the balance in your cash reserve is falling, it's time to take a hard look at where you've been spending those emergency funds. Are those expenses truly important? Or are they expenses that you can budget for and buy down the line?

Delayed gratification might sound unappealing, but it has actually been proven to increase the level of enjoyment one gets from the purchase of budgeted-for items, those that aren't simply impulse buys. And when you get accustomed to watching that cash reserve balance grow, you might be surprised at how less appealing the thought of buying the latest technology iterations become. Saving can become addictive. And that's an addiction you want to experience.

Don't get caught short!

Align the Business and Personal

As I mentioned in the Introduction, successful financial management for small business owners is about aligning the business and personal aspects of the 6 Pillars of Financial Success to ensure they work together and complement each other. In terms of cash flow, how well you manage your business cash flow impacts your personal cash flow position and vice versa.

In simple terms, how well your customer collections are managed impacts the level of drawings/salary the business can afford to pay you, as owner, and your lifestyle. When business cash flow is tight, you, the owner, may have to take a pay cut, either temporarily or long term.

Likewise, taking money out of the business every time you need personal funds, because you are not managing your personal cash flow sufficiently, can kill a good business.

So get on the front foot. Tighten up your business cash flow system. Increase the focus on collections and make cash flow management a strength of your business. **The sale is not complete until you are paid.** Give it that level of focus.

Likewise, manage your personal cash flow so you live within your means and are comfortable. Pay yourself a set level of drawings or salary that is commercially acceptable and affordable and work within that. This will help your business do what it needs to do and reduce the need to continually put money back into the business when you take too much out. It will also help you to live within your means.

By doing this, you will be able to harness your cash flow. It will not slip between your fingers and you will be able to build your business and your personal wealth more effectively.

Key Points

- Successful individuals and businesses are proactive, not reactive, and always on top of their cash flow.

- Respond to issues and disputes promptly. Addressing unpaid/overdue accounts can strengthen client relationships if you approach it from a customer service perspective – is the customer happy? More often than not, overdue bills are not the result of deliberate delinquency. It's not revenue until you receive payment.

- Establish credit terms and adhere to them firmly with customers who are regularly delinquent. Consider asking for prepayment or deposits with challenging clients.

- Spend only 90% of your income, even less if you can. Deposit all your wages/income into one account – your cash reserve account – and then move your set sum for your daily living expenses into your current, day-to-day account.

- Use you cash reserve account as your 'fuel gauge' or cash flow scoreboard and to control the amount you spend on your less frequent and discretionary expenses. If you spend it all, you'll never build wealth!

7

A: Asset Building and Preservation

Asset management, like cash flow management, builds wealth. Once you address cash flow, harnessing and managing it to grow your cash reserves, these reserves can and should be used to build and preserve your assets. This is important *in* your business, but also *beyond* your business.

One owner I know was very successful at doing this. His logic dictated that by having income-producing assets outside his business, he would feel more secure if something adverse happened to him or his business. His investment assets would get him through any bad patch and sufficiently support his family.

In contrast, another business owner who came to me to plan a successful business exit had not done this. Instead, most of their funds had been ploughed into their business over the years and the bulk of their wealth was 'jackpotted' inside the business. Contrary to paying off, over the years, competition had caught up, and as they neared retirement, they were unable to sell the business at a price that would harvest the funds they had ploughed into it.

Due to competition, globalisation, changes in the market, and new, disruptive technologies, to name just a few, there is no guarantee that you will be able to sell your business at the price you need to and live happily ever after. That is why I keep pressing the point home that you must endeavour to become more and more financially independent of your business over time, so that not all of your eggs are in the same basket.

Having a longer-term vision can help you make sound decisions, ones that build for the future, without painting you into a corner, where you can get stuck.

Business Assets

Your investment in your business is a personal asset as well. The growth in value and the strength of your business is very important.

Asset building is too large a topic to cover in detail here. Instead, we will take a more simplified approach, covering the three primary concepts, and leave you to do further research, or consult a professional financial advisor, on whichever areas pertain to you most. The key business asset areas are:

- Working capital assets
- Capital expenditures/fixed assets
- Goodwill

Assets require substantial investment and you take a risk investing in them, so they need to earn their keep. You need a return above your funding cost (the interest you pay to purchase it or forego on the money invested) and a margin for the risk you take. The higher the risk you take, the higher the return you need to earn.

Working Capital Assets

This relates mainly to your cash in the bank, inventory/stock on hand, and accounts receivable (debtors) – what is normally classified as a current asset in your business balance sheet. Collectively, they are referred to as working capital because they are designed to work for you. You need to turn over your business's inventory, collect accounts receivable, and reuse these funds to make your business more profitable.

Inventory needs to keep turning over. Each dollar in stock represents potential bottom-line profits, so the higher the turnover of your inventory, the better it is for your bottom line.

To keep your accounts receivable working for you, customers need to pay on time and bad debts need to be minimised. Limit the length of your credit terms and charge more to cover your funding costs where you do choose to provide more generous terms. In other words, the price for cash up front should be lower than that for customers enjoying a 90-day credit period. The 90-day credit costs the business at least 5% of sales revenue to cover the funding and administration costs and the risk you take in offering it, i.e., the rate a bank would charge to extend credit, plus an extra amount for having less security than a bank would have.

Review the overdue accounts and the aging of your accounts receivable, and keep it as close to your normal credit terms as you can.

Capital Expenditure/Fixed Assets

Capital expenditure represents an investment in your business. Such an investment needs to generate a return. Often, you look at the payback period for this expenditure, which means the amount of time it takes for the profits created by the capital expenditure to pay for the expenditure itself.

For example, say you buy a machine to make donuts. You know roughly the number of donuts your business can sell and the profit to be made. If the machine costs $16,000 and you can make an annual profit of $5,000 on the increased number of donut sales the machine yields versus what you can manage with your current process, the machine has a calculated payback period of just over three years ($16,000/$5,000 = 3.20).

Larger companies and businesses have people dedicated to perform this kind of analysis. ROI (return on investment), discounted cash flow, and a number of other evaluation ratios are used to assess investment and capital expenditure proposals. The payback period is a simple one to use. Talk to your accountant about which one might best suit your business.

Always be sure to assess the proposal and make sure it stacks up before you go ahead with a capital expenditure.

Goodwill

Goodwill is an intangible asset, and for some businesses, especially service-orientated businesses, it can be its most valuable asset. Your customer or client base, and their loyalty to your business, is an example of goodwill. All the work you put into your business generally builds goodwill. If you continue to build this asset, it and this can pay big dividends when you sell your business. Having customer contracts or knowhow (secret recipes, patented products or processes, and such) within your business, and systems and procedures which ensure you do not need to do everything, also builds goodwill.

Personal Assets

Harvesting your wealth and building your assets outside your business is vital to establishing financial security. While these assets may not match the return your business generates, they serve to reduce your overall risk and enhance your lifestyle.

Lifestyle Assets

Certain lifestyle assets, such as cars and boats, are depreciating assets and do not necessarily build wealth but may bring heightened enjoyment to your daily living. Additional lifestyle assets, such as your primary residence and other real estate investments, can be effective means to build security, if invested in wisely.

                                    Peter Gialouris

It makes sense to diversify among business, lifestyle, and personal investment assets. As a rule of thumb, you should aim to have more than half of your wealth as investment and business assets. The goal is to have your lifestyle assets, including your primary residence, comprise less than half of your total wealth.

This is difficult for most people, as buying a home is such a big and important move. However, as you near retirement, say, ten years out, you need to build up your investment assets and your business in order to provide a more financially secure future.

Investment Assets

Investment assets are those that either produce income or appreciate in value over time. Such assets in your personal investment portfolio include your superannuation, investment property, shares (stocks), government bonds, term deposits, and investment funds, both managed and index funds, including ETFs (exchange-traded funds) and lifecycle funds.

Some investments, like investment properties, can be dual-purpose assets, ones that are used but also held onto for appreciation. Some parents invest in one or more additional properties because they worry their children may not be able to buy a home when necessary, or they want to retire someplace other than the family home.

The business owner that I mentioned as being so conscious about asset management, made it a priority to own income-producing assets outside his business. That way if something happened to him or his business, they would see him through any bad patch and support his family, giving him greater peace of mind. That is what I want for you.

These assets that you invest in, other than your business, diversify the risk of having everything in one basket, be it your home or business. To qualify as assets, they must generate a favourable investment return. In order to diversity well, you need to map out an investment strategy. It should cover:

- **Asset allocation / diversification:** what you invest in, including cash, bonds, real estate, and shares (domestic and/or international)
- **Income** (interest, rental income, and dividends) and **capital growth** (capital gains)
- **Your risk tolerance:** Investing in a business, shares, and property poses generally a higher risk than investing in safer, more secure assets, like cash and government bonds. With higher risk comes the possibility (but never the guarantee) of higher returns. If higher-risk assets that fluctuate in value worry you, then you have a low tolerance for risk. You want investments that permit you to sleep at night, without worrying, yet provide sufficient long-term financial security
- **Time horizon:** short (0-3 years), medium (3-7 years) or long term (7+ years), and liquidity requirements
- **Direct** investment versus **indirect** (through an investment fund) – your level of knowledge and the need for advice, a second opinion, etc.
- **Gearing:** the level of borrowed money funding the investment; negative gearing strategy and so on
- **Tax:** income and capital gains taxes
- **Who/what owns the asset and its structure**: individual, joint, super fund, a trust, etc.

Let's look at a brief overview of the principles and considerations inherent in developing a sound investment strategy.

Your Investment Plan

Asset and Investment Classes

The table below shows the basic features and some of the potential risks associated with each asset class.

Asset Class	Features	Risks
Cash	Capital (principal) is safe relative to other asset classes; immediate access to funds.	No inflation protection; low returns expected in the long term; returns fully taxable.
Fixed Interest	Generally secure; guaranteed rate of return.	Interest rates fluctuate, affecting the value or the relative performance of fixed income investments.
Shares	Historically offer growth above inflation long term; growing income; may offer tax benefits; liquid; easy to sell a portion to raise capital. Can diversify internationally; some offer dividend reinvestment plans.	Stock market volatility could lead to losses if forced to sell; market slumps can be prolonged; companies can under-perform or go out of business.
Property	Capital value and income generally rise with inflation; possible tax benefits; provides the emotional security of 'bricks and mortar'.	May be difficult to liquidate in an emergency; typically not possible to sell a portion of the asset when there is a need to raise capital; possible tenant problems; requires hands-on management by owner or management company; sizeable capital concentrated in a single asset.
Alternatives	Includes assets that do not trade on an organised exchange or are otherwise difficult to directly access for the average investor, e.g., commodities, natural resources, private equity, and venture capital; and strategies involving common asset classes (generally via a hedge fund employing global macro, long-short equity, or event-driven strategies); generally very low correlation to traditional portfolio returns.	Investment timeframe is generally medium to long term as the strategies can be illiquid; comfort with the managers (hedge funds) is important, as the process is complex and not transparent; products are high cost; includes a performance fee; single hedge fund strategy is potentially more rewarding but far riskier than a fund-of-funds approach; potentially good diversification benefits.

Below are some risks an investor faces when investing in different markets.

Interest rate	When relying on fixed-rate investments, reinvestment of maturing money may occur at a time when interest rates have fallen significantly
Currency	Currency fluctuations and volatility
Gearing	Borrowing to finance investment acquisitions – in a rising market, gearing can increase returns; in falling markets, financial loss may occur
Legislative	Subject to changes in current laws and regulations, e.g., GST and changing superannuation rules; as legislation alters, this may impact and derail set strategies
Market	Market fluctuations can increase/decrease the value of an investment suddenly, or over time
Lack of diversification	All capital is affected if a single investment does badly – too many eggs in one basket
Mismatch	When the chosen investment is unsuited to the needs and circumstances of the investor (e.g., high-risk for a low-risk-tolerance investor)
Inflation	An undesirable drop in purchasing power when an investment fails to keep pace with inflation
Market timing	Anticipating market rises and falls is extremely difficult, even for sophisticated, knowledgeable investors
Liquidity	Inability to access money quickly or without cost when necessary, such as when an emergency arises
Credit	Associated with debt-type investments, such as debentures and bonds, where the institution invested in may be unable to make the necessary interest payments or repay your funds

Elements of the above tables are drawn from *The Trade-Off: Understanding Investment and Risk*, a joint publication of the Financial Planning Association and Macquarie Investment Management Limited.

The first step in establishing a suitable investment strategy for yourself is to take a moment to identify precisely what your investment objectives are. Here are a few factors to consider.

Your Investment Objectives

- **Portfolio Objective:** What are your reasons for setting up this investment portfolio? Is it to save up a deposit to buy a property? To fund your lifestyle, be it short term or long term? To fund the next generation? Super funds, for example, are designed to provide retirement benefits for their members and, in the event of the death of a member, to provide benefits for the member's dependants and other beneficiaries as per the member's instructions to the trustee.

- **Investment Returns:** What investment returns – what level of income or capital growth or real return (above inflation) – do you seek, and over what period? It could be to achieve an income return equal to the Reserve Bank Cash Rate over a rolling three-year period and a total real return (return above CPI, Australia's Consumer Price Index) of 2% over a rolling five-year period. (As discussed later in this chapter and in Appendix C which contains projected long-term returns and actual (historical) return variances/volatility to help you estimate this.)

- **Liquidity:** Immediate access to investment funds, with little or no penalty for withdrawal, to meet benefit payments and other obligations as they fall due, or to protect in the event of emergency situations.

Once you have identified the objectives that drive this particular investment fund, it is time to determine your investment strategy. An investment strategy takes into consideration not just your objectives but also your investment appreciation targets and the inherent risks associated with the various options. With the potential for high returns comes high risk. The safer the investment option, typically the lower the average annual return.

Your Investment Strategy

Agreed risk profile – Risk tolerance varies from investor to investor, with the rule of thumb being that the sooner you need to access your investment funds, the greater the need to protect the principal invested, which means that high-risk investments that can deplete capital are not good choices for people investing for the short term, unless they can afford the potential loss. For example, you may be comfortable taking risks with your retirement savings if retirement is 30 or more years away versus a mere five years away. That said, not everyone feels comfortable taking the same level of risk, no matter how long the overall investment period is.

A qualified financial planner can supply you with a risk tolerance questionnaire, or you can find one online. For example, if you are assessed as 'moderately conservative', it suggests that you seek some potential for capital growth but prefer to avoid large fluctuations in short-term performance. Based on this risk profile, you would seek a diversified portfolio with a balance of defensive assets such as fixed interest and cash, and growth assets such as shares and property. A 40–60% exposure to growth (higher-risk) assets, such as property and shares, represents a significant risk of your portfolio decreasing in value in the short term, but this risk reduces on average for investments held over the minimum recommended investment term of three years. (Source: Lifespan Financial Planning.)

Diversification and higher-quality investments – Diversification, which is defined as spreading your investment in quality assets among a number of asset classes ranging from low to high risk, exposes you to market gains when the market is strong while protecting against undue volatility (hedging against risk) in order to achieve your average return objective. A combination of asset classes provides potential liquidity, income, a real (above inflation) return, capital security, and tax benefits.

Your Investment Approach

Direct investments are where you directly purchase investment property, company shares (equities), term deposits, and government bonds. You directly own the asset and are the 'investment manager' and usually wholly responsible for your investments.

Indirect investments are where you buy units in a managed fund that invests in the type of assets you would like to invest in. The fund is the investment manager. If you prefer to invest in real estate but want diversification, for example, you might invest in a REIT, a real estate investment trust that owns multiple properties, and multiple types of property, in various locations. Super funds generally invest in managed funds. Whilst someone else is responsible for managing the fund, it is still your responsibility to ensure that its performance continues to adhere to your objectives and strategy.

Passive management – Here you invest in an index fund that mimics an investment index like the ASX, the Australia Securities Exchange, or the S&P 500 in the US, for example, by investing in the very same shares that comprise that particular index. An index fund exposes you to a large variety of shares to provide diversification, and your return mirrors the performance of the index itself. Exchange-traded funds (ETFs) are another type of index-style investment available to individual investors. ETFs generally offer higher daily liquidity and lower fees than traditional managed funds.

Active management – Unlike index funds, actively managed funds are run by financial professionals who actively follow the market and buy and sell shares in the fund on your behalf, based on an investment strategy outlined in the fund's prospectus. As an individual investor, you have no say in terms of what assets are bought and sold, or when. Actively managed funds are more expensive than passively managed funds, so they need to add sufficient value above expenses to justify your investment in them.

Dynamic/tactical asset allocation – This is a heavily managed approach, known as market timing. Trying to time the market, attempting to pick markets that will perform based on current economic and market factors. This is difficult and requires a crystal ball to accurately predict the future, something that even the most skilled, sophisticated investors often fail to do.

Investment returns over time are influenced by strategic asset allocation (e.g., growth (property and shares) versus defensive (cash and fixed interest/bond) investments), security selection (the specific securities owned, either by you or the fund you invest in), and market timing (which market sectors are strong versus weak, and how they respond to, or are influenced by, changes in political, economic, and environmental factors).

Time Horizon

Your investment time horizon also influences the potential for positive return. Time horizons are generally divided into three categories: short-term (0-3 years), medium-term (3-7 years) and long-term (over 7 years) periods. Short- and medium-term portions provide capital access and liquidity and need to be managed on a more strategic and tactical basis to protect capital.

The following table shows how a portfolio can be managed this way, by investing 30% of your assets in short-term-orientated investments, another 30% in medium-term, and the remaining 40% in long-term-orientated investments.

Asset Classes	Short-Term (0-3 years)	Medium-Term (3-7 years)	Long-Term (7+ years)	Total
Australian Equities		5%	20%	25%
International Equities		5%	10%	15%
Property			10%	10%
Alternatives				
Growth Exposure	0%	10%	40%	50%
Australian Fixed Interest	15%	5%		20%
International Fixed Interest		10%		10%
Alternatives				
Cash	15%	5%		20%
Defensive Exposure	30%	20%	0%	50%
Total	30%	30%	40%	100%

Asset mix and asset class allocation – After considering the above objectives and factors, in particular the level of risk, benefit of diversification, and liquidity requirements, determine your investment strategy. e.g.:

Asset Classes	Lower Ranges	Upper Ranges	Strategic Asset Allocation
Australian Equities	10%	35%	25%
International Equities	5%	24%	15%
Property	0%	16%	10%
Alternatives	0%	0%	0%
Growth Exposure	15%	70%	50%
Australian Fixed Interest	17%	55%	20%
International Fixed Interest	8%	36%	10%
Alternatives	0%	0%	0%
Cash	5%	60%	20%
Defensive Exposure	30%	85%	50%

Expected Long-Term Average Gross Income & Growth for Individual Asset Classes

Asset Class	Working Long-Term Gross Returns		
	Income %	Growth %	Total Return %
Australian Shares	4	5	9
International Shares	2	7	9
Property Securities	6	2	8
Australian Fixed Interest	5	1	6
International Fixed Interest	5	1	6
Cash	5	0	5
Inflation (CPI)			3

Source: Lifespan Financial Planning Pty Ltd. Please note that these income and growth rates are based on projected future performance, and are intended only as a guide to likely returns over the medium to long term (over 5 years) and should be treated with caution. (Refer to Appendix C for the volatility (historical annual return variances) of these asset classes).

Excluded Investments

Some investments that may not be suitable, based on your investment objectives, risk profile, and strategy, could include:

- Hedge funds – these often lack transparency and are generally high risk
- Highly geared funds, such as those with an LVR (loan-to-value ratio) above 25%
- Funds heavily invested in derivative instruments (unless designed to protect the fund)
- Funds with excessive performance fees and where annual performance bonuses are paid to investment managers

There are always costs associated with investing:

1. **Upfront transaction costs** – Trading fees levied by brokers or fund managers when you buy and sell some or your entire investment, and stamp duty on property purchases and selling costs, are examples of standard transaction fees.

2. **Administrative costs** – These include recordkeeping, preparing tax information, trust management expenses, and super fund costs, and vary depending on the type of investments you hold.

3. **Investment Management** – Costs associated with the actual managing of the investment, whether you do it yourself or use a professional manager. It can range from a flat fee or percentage or, as in the case with an investment property, actual operating expenses/maintenance costs, in addition to insurance and capital expenditures.

4. **Advisory fees** – Your accountant, investment/financial advisor, lawyer, or any other professional advisor.

These costs can quickly add up and ideally should be funded by your investment return while leaving you sufficient return to achieve your objectives. Costs should be weighed against the benefit(s) they provide you. Benefits can include the savings in time and effort of you doing the work yourself, any added value that professional expertise provides, including guidance on quality investments and choices best suited to your particular situation, and the potential for higher returns with lower risk.

More detailed information on how to craft an investment strategy can be found at the back, in Appendix C. I encourage you to familiarise yourself with it before making any decisions or sitting down with an investment advisor.

Periodic Review and Re-balancing

Just like your regular cash flow review, investment portfolios benefit from regular review. Markets fluctuate, your situation changes over time, lifestyle changes such as the birth of a child, can influence your investment goals – all these must be taken into consideration when reviewing your portfolio. The more active a management role you play, the more frequently you should review the portfolio.

Passive management of long-term investments in quality investment structures can be done once or twice a year, but investments in actively managed portfolios, or in properties where you or the property manager you hire are responsible for the day-to-day management, should be reviewed by you or your accountant on a quarterly, monthly, or even weekly basis as appropriate.

If you are unsure how to start investing, or what type of investing suits your circumstances best, it is always advisable to obtain professional advice, counsel, and assistance from an independent financial investment professional, one who is not biased or heavily influenced by commissions or limited in terms of offering only what their company sells.

Business and Investment Structures

Asset Protection Against Liabilities

Typically, when you own an asset as an individual, or in a joint/partnership situation, each individual is personally liable for any and all losses, claims, and liabilities. In order to provide asset protection from such liabilities, ownership of assets can be transferred into one or more structures that protect against personal liability. If assets are to be held jointly/in partnership, a partnership agreement should be drawn up by a lawyer and you will need to complete partnership tax returns in addition to your individual one.

Company-Held Assets

If your assets are held by a company, a separate legal entity with limited liability, those assets enjoy more protection, although in certain circumstances company directors can assume personal liability. Assets are held in the company's name, and the company manages and controls the assets. Set-up and ongoing costs are generally higher than those associated with joint/partnership structures, with set-up costs generally around $1,000 and ongoing costs contingent upon how active the company is.

Always consult an accountant or lawyer before attempting to transfer asset ownership into a company to ensure the appropriate protections and desired advantages are available to you.

Trust-Held Assets

The same is true for a trust, which can own assets and afford increased asset protection from creditors. Assets are held in the trustee's name, and the trustee manages and controls the assets. Always consult a professional for advice before setting up a legally binding trust.

Set-up costs for trusts generally run about $1,500, while on-going costs vary depending on how active the trust is and whether there are individual trustees or a corporate trustee in place.

Super Fund-Held Assets

You can also transfer assets into super funds (subject to the rules), where in most cases they are protected from personal liability by individuals, including members. The assets are held in the name of the super fund's trustee, and that trustee manages and controls the assets. As with trust and company structures, legal advice is recommended before taking action.

Setting up a self-managed super fund (SMSF) usually costs about $1,500; ongoing costs vary depending on how the fund is structured. Super funds are subject to special rules which add to their complexity and ongoing costs.

More detailed information on business and investment structures can be found at the back, in Appendix B. I encourage you to study this information carefully.

The Bottom Line

Planning your investment strategy and executing it is not something to be done impulsively or without sufficient careful thought. Some business owners feel comfortable making their own investment decisions while others are more comfortable leaving those decisions to professionals. Regardless of which route you choose, you need to consider what your investment goals and objectives are, use those goals to identify what your liquidity needs are and the time horizon available to you for investment, and calculate what kind of return you need to achieve your objectives. The best strategies are based on sound, accurate information.

Superannuation

Superannuation is a great investment structure. In Australia, it is purpose-built for retirement and boasts tax and asset-protection benefits. Compulsory superannuation contributions mean that almost all Australians possess a super fund, which often becomes our primary source of income in retirement.

An SMSF can be a powerful vehicle for you as a business owner. One reason is that your SMSF can own your business property and your business can lease it from your SMSF at market rent, which is a tax-effective strategy to build up your nest egg for retirement while helping you with the business.

Choosing the right super fund is a bit like choosing a car. There are many brands and types, each as individual as their owners. One size does not fit all. You need to select the one that suits your needs.

- Government and corporate funds (for eligible employees)
- Industry funds
- Retail funds
- Wrap accounts
- Small APRA funds
- SMSF (self-managed super fund)

Each of these has distinct features and fees, some of which may be beneficial to you and some which may not be. Value for money, flexibility, control, and a high level of service are important considerations. The choice you make can seriously affect your retirement, so I urge you to consider getting professional advice before making any decisions.

Your Super Investment Strategy

Your investment plan and the principles covered earlier in this chapter will help you here.

How you choose to invest the money within your fund is important: namely, how much you invest in safer assets, designed to protect your capital, versus riskier, growth-orientated assets. The goal is to generate greater investment returns, after fees and taxes, over decades. Taking calculated risks, avoiding major setbacks, not putting all your eggs in one basket – these decisions require careful deliberation. There are a number of factors to weigh up.

The first is to determine your risk profile – what level of risk are you comfortable with? A qualified financial planner will ask you a series of questions to determine just how comfortable you are with higher-risk investments to ensure that the choices you make are ones you can live with comfortably, without undue stress. As mentioned earlier in the chapter, risk profile assessments can also be found online.

Another consideration is your age and financial position. Are you still building up your investment assets? Are you approaching retirement? Are you drawing a pension?

Other considerations include what specific investments you should have, whether the default fund in your chosen super plan is adequate for your needs, and whether you might want a combination of managed funds and direct investments (term deposits and direct shares, for example), a packaged diversified portfolio (like a balanced fund), or individual sector funds. You also need to decide how much hands-on control you want to have.

Your Insurance Strategy

Most Australians insure their property, namely their car(s) and house/ real estate. Too few, however, have adequate insurance to protect their most important asset – themselves. Your future depends on your ability to work and earn an income over your working life. Without this, you will not be able to achieve the things you plan to. Insurance is a prudent way to cover this risk. Most super funds contain income protection and life & TPD (total & permanent disablement) insurance options. You need to determine just how much cover you need, both for yourself and your family, to ensure that your dependants will be financially secure if something happens to you.

Your Contribution Strategy

Compulsory SG (super guarantee) contributions are unlikely to sufficiently fund you in retirement. You need to calculate how much super you will need, whether you should make additional contributions, what the tax and other considerations are if you do

                                                     Peter Gialouris

this, and how can you ensure that your super will last over the entire duration of your retirement.

An additional 1% each year in investment return, after costs and tax, plus higher contributions, say, an additional 5% of your annual salary could, over time, potentially double your benefit in real terms, after allowing for inflation. Conversely, poor returns, higher fees and charges, and/or lost super benefits from past jobs can cut deeply into your end super benefit.

Making the Right Choices

With all these considerations, and all the available choices, how to invest in super can be a bewildering prospect. The easy option is to use the default superannuation fund for your business, the default investment and insurance options within that fund, and the minimum SG contributions, and then cross your fingers and hope for the best. With luck, this may be adequate, but are you really willing to rely on luck for your eventual livelihood? That would be a huge gamble to take, not just for yourself but also for your family.

The alternative, which I strongly recommend, is to be more proactive and make your own luck. Make the time to learn more about your super, and get professional advice if you need assistance. Make your super work for you. You won't regret it.

Align the Business and Personal

If your major asset is your business, this increases your personal risk. You have all your proverbial eggs in one basket, so if the basket breaks, or you drop it, you stand to lose everything. That is not a risk you want to – or should – take. That said, you can harvest the wealth from your business to buy personal assets such as your home, or build an investment portfolio such as your super, which reduces and spreads that personal risk. Instead of half a dozen eggs in one basket, you now have three baskets, each containing two eggs, cutting your risk of loss potentially by two-thirds.

Also, the way you invest in these assets, your home, super, and other investments, can reduce your risk further. One example of this kind of asset protection strategy was mentioned earlier: having an SMSF own your business property, which, if done wisely, can benefit both you, the business owner, and the business itself. In addition, your super can play a vital role in your retirement strategy. Your business exit strategy should form part of your overall business plan, and the tax considerations and concessions that apply to the sale of your business need to be factored in. We will look at tax strategies and estate plan/exit strategies in the coming chapters, but for now let's take a quick look at one sample scenario.

Let's say you're married, with children, and own your home. You have a plumbing business, complete with staff, you run your business at a business location you call the factory, and you own the property. Your business is very profitable.

Let's look at two simple ownership options for each key asset.

Asset	Values	Option 1	Option 2	Option 2 Benefit
Business	$0.3 million net annual profit after tax	Sole Trader	Company or Trading Trust	Management, Asset Protection, Tax
Business Property	$1 million	Sole Trader	SMSF	Retirement, Asset Protection, Tax
Family Home	$1 million	Jointly with your spouse	Spouse	Asset Protection
Investments	$0.5 million	Jointly with your spouse	SMSF or Family Trust	Management, Asset Protection, Tax

                                      Peter Gialouris

Consult a professional advisor to see which structure(s) can offer you the most benefits long term as well as afford the most asset protection.

Building up your business and ensuring the assets earn their keep makes sense. Building up your lifestyle assets in a measured way also makes sense. Building your investments, including super, with a clear investment strategy, to make you financially independent of your business, will ensure you get more out of your business and set yourself up for life.

Key Points

- Managing and building assets is how you build wealth. The primary focus of your surplus cash flow should be ultimately on acquiring valuable assets to fund your future.

- Determine your risk tolerance and your investment time horizon before making any major investments. When in doubt, always consult a qualified advisor.

- Business assets include working capital assets, fixed/capital assets, and the goodwill you develop with customers to ensure their continued patronage.

- The risks inherent in assets should never outweigh or override their potential value to you. The greater the risk, the greater the return must be to justify owning it.

- Your goal should be to ensure your lifestyle assets, including your home, comprise less than half of your wealth.

- The cost of maintaining an investment should not equal or eclipse any return.

- Asset management is best achieved through regular review, as values, fees/costs, and tax structures are subject to change.

- Who – or what – owns the assets can make a big difference in their ultimate benefit to you. Consult a tax specialist or financial advisor to ensure your decisions are the right ones for you.

8

D: Debt Management

By now, you are on your way to improving cash flow and building a strong asset base. However, debt can erode this wealth, unless you control its negative impact, both in your business and for you personally. If you get on the wrong side of this, it can set you back big time. But it is possible to successfully manage debt in ways that add value.

Not long before writing this book, I sat down with a new client who had secured a bank loan for a business he co-owned. Whilst examining the details, I saw the bank had been given the factory as security (a factory which was worth more than twice the amount of the loan) as well as having levied a charge on the whole business plus personal guarantees from all three owners. I thought, talk about overkill! The factory alone was more than sufficient security for the loan. The personal guarantees not only put the personal assets of all three owners unnecessarily at risk but restricted what else they could do financially, outside the business.

In an attempt to eliminate the risk they take, lenders typically demand more security than is necessary. They will rarely turn to you and say, 'We have too much security' and give some of it back. I immediately set out to correct this for my client. The bank, after some arm wrestling, agreed to reduce the loan's collateral to the factory.

Business

Borrowing money can help you fund and build your business, as long as the borrowed funds are productive and you are in a position to comfortably repay them.

As a general rule, less debt is better than more. The amount you borrow needs to be affordable, especially when things go wrong. If in doubt, borrow less.

Do your homework. Ensure the funds are necessary, and that all alternative, less costly sources have been explored, such as the collection of overdue accounts and sale of excess inventory. Remember the client back in chapter 4, when we discussed cost-benefit analysis, who polled his customers on their salon's renovation plans and it turned out all the customers wanted in the way of improvement was better quality coffee? This is what I'm talking about when I say to do your homework before you borrow, before you spend. Make sure your house is in order. If you are bleeding cash flow, fix that problem first.

There are a number of considerations when borrowing for your business:

- Debt type (e.g., bank overdraft, loan)
- Interest rate, fixed or variable – the closer to the bank overdraft or base rates, the better
- Security required, such as commercial property, home, or other guarantee – reduce the amount of personal assets and personal security you provide as much as possible in order to ensure the business stands on its own and to give you more freedom and opportunity with your personal investment plan
- Features – loans with additional features can be more expensive but also offer greater flexibility; these include interest-only loans, using the asset being financed as security, and more attractive repayment terms

A good bank, along with good banking connections, is very important to small business owners. When you need funds to expand and grow your business, having the bank onside or having accessible finance is vital.

Depending on the business and the situation, your bank may appear to have all the power in the relationship, such as demanding a level of security that exceeds the value of the funds they provide. By working with the bank and negotiating a fairer outcome, this can free you up to do more, creating enhanced growth opportunities for you as well as the business. Determine the fair market value of the assets you will potentially offer for collateral ahead of time, get it in writing, and be ready to present it to the bank officer when negotiating.

Personal

Personal debt needs to be managed in a similar fashion to your business debt. The same basic factors apply here as listed above: debt type, interest rate, the type of security required, and the loan features. Low-interest-rate loans like home loans tend to offer fewer features. Some features, like a mortgage offset account, can be useful. Negotiate to include the features you need, such as redraw facilities, early repayment options without break penalties, greater flexibility and options, and/or lower fees.

In addition to these features, there are other considerations when contemplating personal debt. One is whether the interest on the loan is tax-deductible or not. If the loan is for an income-producing purpose, the interest expense is generally tax-deductible. (Business debt and investment loans fall into this category.) Where the loan is for a private or non-income-producing purpose, the interest expense is not tax-deductible (e.g. a home loan). Deductible debt is obviously more tax effective. It is always worthwhile to consider this when you borrow funds and structure your debt in order to maximise those borrowings which are tax-deductible.

The amount you borrow is naturally a prime consideration. The less you borrow, the better overall, but make sure you borrow enough so that you do not restrict or stretch yourself or deplete capital unnecessarily. Just avoid flying too high or getting in too deep.

Yet another issue to consider is who (or what) should own the asset. It usually depends on the purpose of the loan – home, investment, etc. Issues that influence this decision include:

1. Income and capital gains taxes.

2. Asset protection – professionals or business owners who bear professional liability or business risks should carefully consider ownership of personal assets when the risk of loss affects the family, such as risking the family home.

3. Ease of administration – some ways of owning assets can involve initial setup and ongoing administration and accounting fees but may also be easier to administer. A family trust, for example, can be a powerful intergenerational vehicle for an investment asset like an investment property or direct shares that you want to retain in the family.

4. Intended use – some personal use assets, like a family residence or vacation/second home will not work for you if your super fund owns it. The super fund can become non-compliant, resulting in having to pay tax at the top tax rate on the whole fund versus the lower super fund concessional tax rate.

Align the Business and Personal

There are a number of key overlap areas here that can add value and make life easier if they are aligned.

- **Business debt and personal security** – The personal assets and guarantees you provide as security increases your personal risk and restricts what you can do outside your business. A qualified professional (accountant, lawyer or financial advisor) can discuss asset protection strategies that can help.
- **Mortgage offset and cash flow management** – These allow you to offset your personal surplus funds against your home loan, which is tax effective, pays the home loan interest rate on the these funds, and funds are accessible to you for money management purposes.
- **Tax** – It is important to make any debt tax effective, to get a tax deduction for the interest whenever possible. Business and investment loans are usually deductible, while home and personal loans for a car or travel are generally not tax-deductible.
- **Insurance** – Insurance can cover debt when things go wrong, such as if you die or become disabled, either temporarily or permanently, and find yourself unable to work.

Key Points

- Debt erodes wealth unless managed properly.

- Never provide more security than necessary.

- Maximise borrowings that are tax-deductible.

9

T: Tax Strategies

In addition to debt liabilities, tax also erodes wealth. It can wield a significant impact both on your business cash flow and profitability and the lifestyle you maintain using your personal cash flow.

When I left university in 1979, fiddling one's taxes was considered to be a national sport. Over the years, the ATO (Australian Taxation Office) has clamped down on excesses. Most tax agents now focus on compliance rather than promoting tax schemes. These days, the risks for noncompliance are too high – huge fines and even jail terms.

These days, minimising your tax on an annual basis is a good initial step. However, using tax-effective strategies that work over the long term or not becoming too obsessed about tax and being more focused on maximising your after-tax returns is more productive.

Most of the short-sighted tax strategies that come to mind involve a commercial property and/or negative gearing. I know of two couples that were not given good advice. In both cases, commercial property was involved which could have been transferred into their SMSF (self-managed superannuation fund) prior to retirement. Instead, both couples ended up unnecessarily paying significantly more tax in retirement.

Similar issues can arise with negative gearing strategies. This generally results in the investment asset and related loan being in the name of the person with the highest marginal tax rate. When this person wants to sell the property or gets closer to retirement, this can become a millstone, often costing the owner all the past tax savings in higher capital gains tax or necessitating paying higher tax in retirement.

Another potentially disastrous strategy is not declaring all your income or engaging in tax avoidance. There are plenty of ways – all legal – to potentially lower your tax burden. Arming yourself with the right information is the best way to accomplish this.

In running a business, accurate numbers and using legal ways to minimise your tax is the smart way to go. Understating your taxable business income, especially through not recording cash monies, carries four primary risks:

- **Staff** – Some, if not all, usually know what's going on. This puts you as the owner of the business at a disadvantage. A tip-off to the ATO from an aggrieved ex-staff member can cause you plenty of grief.
- **Business exit** – When you sell the business, you cannot get full value when you have concealed how profitable the business is. I have heard of cases where businesses prepared two sets of books. Even then, a buyer is reluctant to believe the second set. So the savings in tax can be reduced by the goodwill lost on sale.
- **Bottom line accuracy** – You can lose track of precisely how well, or poorly, the business is going.
- **Tax penalties** – Once you're caught by the ATO, financial ruin is often the consequence.

Be smart. Run a good, honest business, keep accurate records, minimise your tax legally, and maximise after-tax results. If you are not sure how to maximise your after-tax options, consult an accountant or tax specialist.

Basic Tax Structures and Rates

Rates stated below are current at the time of writing this book; however, rates will change over time. Make sure you always stay up to date on current tax rates and how they affect your specific situation before making any financial decisions.

A discount of 50% of capital gains on assets and investments held for more than 12 consecutive months applies to all of the structures listed below *except* a company (which gets no discount) and super funds (which are governed by different rules and receive a CGT discount of one-third). The same 50% discount applies to trust beneficiaries in the trust category and may not apply to a trust itself. The key rates are:

- **Individual** – Individual marginal tax rates (MTR) apply. The top marginal tax rate is currently 49%, while capital gains tax (CGT) varies based on your MTR, with a 50% discount on assets and investments held for more than one year.

- **Joint/Partnership** – Individual tax rates of the owners apply (see above).

- **Company** – The current corporate tax rate is 30% (slightly less for qualifying small businesses). A company can pay shareholders 'franked' dividends (which include the tax paid, and is a tax credit for the shareholder) where the tax paid by the company is passed on to the shareholder, who pays the difference between that 30% corporate rate and their MTR. If their MTR is lower than 30%, the Government refunds the individual the difference. As explained above, a company is not eligible for the 50% CGT discount.

- **Trust** – Individual tax rates of the beneficiaries apply (see Individual above, including CGT discount).

- **Super fund/SMSF** – 15% income tax and 10% CGT in the accumulation phase; 0% tax in the pension phase under the $1.6m pension cap (a new development at the time of writing).

Business

There are a number of business taxes, the primary ones being income tax, company tax, capital gains tax (CGT), goods and services tax (GST), and payroll tax. Accurate records, good tax advice, and solid tax planning go a long way to keep you safely within the tax rules and minimise the impact of these taxes.

Paying more tax than necessary and being levied penalties due to errors or mistakes are obviously things you want to avoid. Likewise, being obsessed about tax is not healthy either. Maximising your after-tax return and having a longer-term approach should be your goals.

One shining light for small business owners are small business tax concessions. These concessions are very useful for business owners nearing retirement, when they sell their business. There are also capital gains tax exemptions to maximise your after-tax sale price, and higher superannuation contribution limits to consider, which should be factored into your exit and retirement strategies.

Many small business owners miss out on these concessions. A leading tax and superannuation expert in Australia stated that *nine out of ten small-business owners who sell their business do not use these concessions.* (It appears that these concessions are not widely used, as business owners or their advisors do not fully understand the opportunity to access this tax relief.) That's just throwing money away, money that could be used in retirement instead of handed unnecessarily to the government. These tax concessions exist to lower your tax burden. Ask your tax accountant about tax concessions and how they may apply to your situation.

Personal

Minimising tax up front is worthwhile, but maximising after-tax returns is even smarter. Tax is an important consideration but don't obsess about it.

We all have heard of high-income earners who sink money into an avocado farm or similar tax scheme that boasts an upfront tax break, and when the scheme fails, they lose all their money. To potentially save up to 50% in tax, they are prepared to lose one 100% of their money. That does not make sense to me. Why not pay an accounting, tax, or business consulting fee and get a tax deduction that way? Or invest in a better project, one that will maximise your after-tax outcome?

It is difficult to reduce your tax substantially without taking a longer-term tax planning approach. Legitimate tax strategies worth examining include:

- **Negative gearing** – You borrow money to buy an investment that generates a tax loss after interest costs and a tax benefit. For this strategy to succeed you need a good investment providing capital growth in the long run and you need to be able to pay the interest and any other associated expenses. If this is not achieved, it can be costly. Also, depending on who/what owns the asset, any tax benefits risk being eaten up by capital gains tax when the asset is sold.
- **Structures** – The common ones are individual/sole trader, joint/partnership, company, and trust. These can have different income and capital gains tax treatments. Using the right structure can yield valuable tax benefits, but you, or your advisor, need to keep on top of this as the tax laws and rules can change and significantly affect the tax treatment.

- **Superannuation** – This is currently a concessionally taxed investment fund for your retirement nest egg. Concessional super contributions provide a tax benefit; however, the rules keep changing in this area, which is a nuisance for long-term planning. Being proactive through an ongoing advice and review process is the best way to manage this. Don't ignore this valuable option.

All too often, without professional advice beforehand, an investment asset is purchased and negatively geared in the name of the person with the highest income and tax. As they approach retirement, they want to sell the asset to get the funds into super, which is a concessionally taxed vehicle for retirement. (The tax rate in the pension phase is nil at the time of writing, up to the $1.6m pension cap). They either sell the asset and pay a larger amount in CGT, relinquishing most of the tax benefits received in tax payments, or they don't want to pay the CGT and end up paying more tax in retirement. I have seen cases where people find themselves paying the top marginal tax rate in retirement, which is currently close to 50%, whereas in super it would be significantly less, sometimes 0%. Which would you rather pay?

This area is very complex, and professional advice from a qualified lawyer, accountant, or financial planner is recommended. Good tax and legal advice, along with a long-term approach, is invaluable when exploring strategic tax options. With the right advice, you can avoid the mistake of investing in the wrong name or structure and paying for it in retirement. Avoid the temptation to wing it. Get expert advice.

For more information on tax considerations, see the chart in Appendix B at the back of the book.

Align the Business and Personal

There are a number of key overlap areas here that can add value and make life easier if they align.

- **Business and personal cash flow** – This can be as simple as failing to put sufficient funds aside to pay the tax bill. It can also depend on your tax structure. For sole traders, when business booms, it can create tax headaches for the owner. These are arguably good problems to have because you're making money. It is better to keep one step ahead of these issues.
- **Mortgage offset and cash flow management** – Mortgage offset allows you to offset your personal surplus funds against your home loan. Interest expense on your home loan is offset against your interest income from the mortgage offset so you do not pay tax on that interest income. Being a personal, non-income producing asset, the interest expense on your home loan is not tax-deductible. Overall, the practice is tax effective. (See the previous chapter on managing debt for more details.)
- **Debt and tax** –Tax-deductible debt relates to your business and investment loans. Because they are being used for income-producing purposes, the interest expense is generally tax-deductible. (See the previous chapter on managing debt for more details.)
- **Small business tax concessions and retirement strategy** – These can reduce your tax on the sale of your business and increase the amount you can put into super for your retirement. This is designed to help small business owners when they retire or sell their business.
- **Company tax** – Franking credits are created when your company pays tax on its profits. Due to dividend imputation,

when a franked dividend is paid to you as the shareholder in the company, you receive a portion of the tax your company has paid, which you can claim in your tax return, reducing your personal tax liability. It was introduced to avoid 'double taxation' of income. So if your company tax rate is 30% and your marginal tax rate (MTR) is 30%, you pay no extra tax on that income. If your MTR is 49%, you pay 19% in tax (MTR less company tax). If your MTR is below 30%, even as low as 0%, you get the tax refunded back to you (0% less 30%).

Key Points

- Always stay on the right side of the law! The penalties for tax avoidance can be devastating.

- Be sure to consider the small business tax concessions – 90% of all small business owners overlook these, which is like throwing away money.

- Tax strategies should focus more on the long term rather than just what might provide immediate or short term savings.

- Tax laws change and are quite complex. This is one area where consulting a skilled tax specialist is a smart investment.

10

R: Risk, Protecting Your Downside

Risk management is a wealth-protecting strategy designed to help you to reduce your exposure to both business and personal risk.

Business

A hairdresser who ran a number of salons had an unfortunate setback. In addition to cutting clients' hair, he managed the salons by visiting one each day and ensuring the staff were productive and that the salons were being run properly and making money. Business was going well. However, he carried substantial debt to fund the expansion of his business, debt that was secured by his home, a common occurrence amongst small business owners.

One day, he injured his back and was unable to work for six months. By the time he returned to work, he only had one salon left and had barely managed to keep his house. Had he taken the time to set up a Plan B and certain systems and procedures, it would have reduced his risk and the fallout. Instead, the business was too dependent on the owner and having so much debt only increased his risk.

In contrast, the owner of a fruit shop suffered an injury one day when a forklift ran over his foot, which put him unexpectedly out of action for a number of months. Buying and selling the right produce at the right price is a key factor in running a successful fruit shop business, as is the connections and relationships amongst market suppliers. The injured owner was the main buyer. Thanks to sufficient advance planning, his family was able to cover for him and the business survived the short-term setback.

Risk management measures, such as adequate insurance cover like key person and business expenses insurance, reduce this kind of impact and help you weather this kind of rough patch. Developing staff so that they, and the business, are less dependent on you, the owner, is also advisable. While insurance can admittedly be a rather dry area, I encourage you to read this chapter carefully.

Areas you should consider addressing are as follows:

1. **Control** – Take calculated risks that you can cover or recover from if they do not pay off. Think like an investor, not a gambler.
2. **Measures** – Cover your downside risks where you can, like IT (information technology), computer security, regular system backups, disaster recovery plans, steps to protect your IP (intellectual property), knowhow, and sensitive information. Go the extra mile here. Losses in these areas are often self-inflicted, the result of neglect, and in most cases preventable.
3. **Insurance** – In addition to doing all you can in practical terms, use insurance to protect your other big risks – the gaps. Some suggested insurance includes:
   - **General insurance** – for your premises (theft, fire, flood, etc.), inventory, public liability, workers compensation, and business interruption. Consult your insurance broker regarding what kind of coverage suits your individual situation.
   - **Key person insurance** – Protects against the negative effect the loss of a key person will have on the income and

value of your business. Cover should include you *and* all key employees.

- **Buy/Sell insurance** – This kind of insurance is accompanied by an agreement between business partners who agree to buy out another partner's interest in the business should certain devastating events, such as death, disability, divorce, or bankruptcy occur, or if a partner retires and wants to sell. This cover is particularly important when a business has more than one owner. It also protects the owner's family if the owner dies or becomes disabled. The BuySell insurance links the owners' agreement to related life insurance policies and provides funds to the surviving owners to buyout the owner who has died or become disabled.

- **Business expenses insurance** – This short-term disability insurance covers fixed business expenses in the event you are taken ill or disabled, covering the business's rent, utilities, staff wages, and other regular expenses necessary to keep your business running in your absence. Typically, these policies are limited to 12 months or less.

Personal

Managing personal risk is just as important as managing business risk. As with your business, you should embrace any practical measures you can take to protect you, your family, and your personal property. Insurance is a proven and effective way to cover your personal risk exposures. Examples of risk management measures include:

1. **Business risk** – You are exposed to the creditor and bankruptcy risk of your business, meaning that if the business

fails, you may be personally liable for some, and possibly all, of the shortfall. There are asset protection strategies available to you to minimise this risk, such as using company and trust structures where relevant and beneficial.

2. **General insurance** – Home building and contents, motor vehicle, public liability, health cover, etc.

3. **Personal insurance cover** – In addition to insurance to protect your business, you need adequate personal insurance to protect you and your family. This includes:

   - Life insurance, which pays your estate or designated beneficiary a lump sum payment upon your death. This lump sum payment can be used to repay debts or invested to provide ongoing income for your family.

   - TPD (total and permanent disablement), which pays a lump sum if you suffer an illness or injury that permanently and completely prevents you from working again. This type of insurance is often implemented as an extension to a life insurance policy to potentially reduce the overall cost of insurance. (You may be able to choose, if eligible, between 'own occupation' and 'any occupation' cover. The first protects you if you are unable to continue to work in your own occupation, regardless of whether you are unable to work in any other occupation, and commands a higher premium cost as a result. Whereas the second pays benefits if you are unable to work in any occupation whatsoever. The latter carries a lower annual premium cost because it is less common for policyholders to be deemed unable to work in any occupation for which they are suited by education, training, and/or experience.)

- Income protection insurance, which typically pays up to 75% of your income if you are unable to work through illness or injury. You can choose a waiting period of between two weeks and two years before cover commences. (If you can afford to wait to collect, electing to take a longer waiting period before benefits kick in reduces the premiums. You can also choose to be covered for a specific period, such as two or five years, or to age 65. For the income protection cover, you may have the option to choose between agreed value, which is based on your income level at policy initiation, and indemnity benefits, which are based on your income level at the time of disablement. The advantage with the agreed value policy is that you know how much you will receive. Because of this, the premiums for the agreed value option will be higher. Those with variable income levels, such as self-employed, are most often better served by the agreed value benefit, while traditional salary-based earners, whose wages generally increase steadily over time, are better protected by an indemnity benefit.)

- Trauma/critical illness insurance provides a lump sum payment in the event that you suffer a critical medical condition or injury as defined within the insurance policy. Examples of critical conditions commonly included in policy conditions are heart attack, stroke, and cancer. The payment is made regardless of whether you are able to resume work and it can relieve financial pressure at a time when you are under great stress. Exercise care when choosing an insurer, as company definitions of medical conditions vary significantly.

Many people forget that professionals, like certain doctors, dentists, and barristers, are, in essence, business owners. Years ago, a high-income-earning barrister came to see me, wanting his personal insurance reviewed. He had a high income, substantial cover, and substantial debts, because he had a large family, all going through school at that stage. I determined that the bulk of his cover took care of the bank, but not his family. We needed to increase his cover in selected areas to address the gaps.

Using insurance is an effective way to protect against the downside. Make sure your advisor is qualified, experienced, and trustworthy, one who looks after you.

Align the Business and Personal

There are a number of key overlap areas here that can add value and make life easier if they align.

1. **Your business risk** – Understanding your personal exposure and adopting strategies to control and minimise this risk is prudent. This is not about avoiding obligations or responsibilities; it is about avoiding being the target or easy option in a distress situation. Why should selling your home be the first port of call? Why not exhaust the business options first?

2. **Business and personal cover** – The cover you, as owner, have in your business: Business Expenses, Key Person, Buy/Sell, and how this relates to your personal cover: life, TPD, and income protection. Cover the gaps and make sure they fit and work together efficiently.

3. **Personal insurance** – You must decide whether to take this cover out within your super fund or split the policy. There are

a number of pros and cons here to consider, including possible tax-deductibility of premiums.

4. **Tax-deductible premiums and taxable proceeds** – This is a very complex area. Get good tax advice so you know where you stand. Paying more tax than you need to due to poor planning can really hurt when you or your family need the funds the most.

5. **An estate plan in the event of illness or injury** – This dovetails with the control of your business. If you are unable to make decisions due to illness or injury, your estate planning documents control who acts on your behalf. In cases where this is not in place or not done correctly, the business can be hamstrung and vulnerable.

6. **Your estate plan and insurance** – can interrelate. If you own the policy or have nominated your estate as the beneficiary of your life insurance policy, the proceeds will form part of your Will. Whether these proceeds form part of your estate or are paid directly to your preferred beneficiary needs to be carefully considered.

Your Insurance Plan

Although insurance is a well-established and proven business and personal protection tool/strategy, it is a specialised area and the fine print matters. Be careful and ensure you get good advice. Triple-check that you are covered for everything you need, especially when you change policies. Ensure that when you make the change to a new policy, you are fully covered from day one versus there being an initial period where you may not have full cover. Know the full disclosure rules to ensure you provide 'full disclosure' to the insurance company when answering the medical, occupation, lifestyle etc. questions on the application form and right up to the policy being issued. You are required to do this so the insurance company can fully assess the risk involved in providing the insurance cover to you. Otherwise, your cover may not be locked in due to your non-disclosure.

The insurance cover outlined above is part of an overall strategy. You need to watch the gaps and manage the overlaps. For example, income protection cover is unlikely to cover 100% of your current net income, as 75–85% is generally the maximum. That means you will need a capital sum from your TPD or trauma cover if you need to bridge that gap. Likewise, income protection cover generally ends by age 65, although some policies can run longer. Again, you might need a capital sum from your TPD or trauma cover to bridge the income shortfall or your funding after age 65.

Another factor that potentially impacts the level of cover you require is your investment assets. Your income-producing assets, like shares and investment property, your realisable (non-lifestyle) assets, and your superannuation fund all can assist to cover the above risks, so the insurance cover you require can be reduced by the level of investment and super assets you have.

If you are financially independent, meaning you have sufficient investment and super assets to support your income needs, then you do not need personal insurance cover (TPD, income protection, trauma, or even life insurance). You will still need general insurance to cover your property and general insurance risks, however. If you already have personal insurance, that, too, needs to be allowed for.

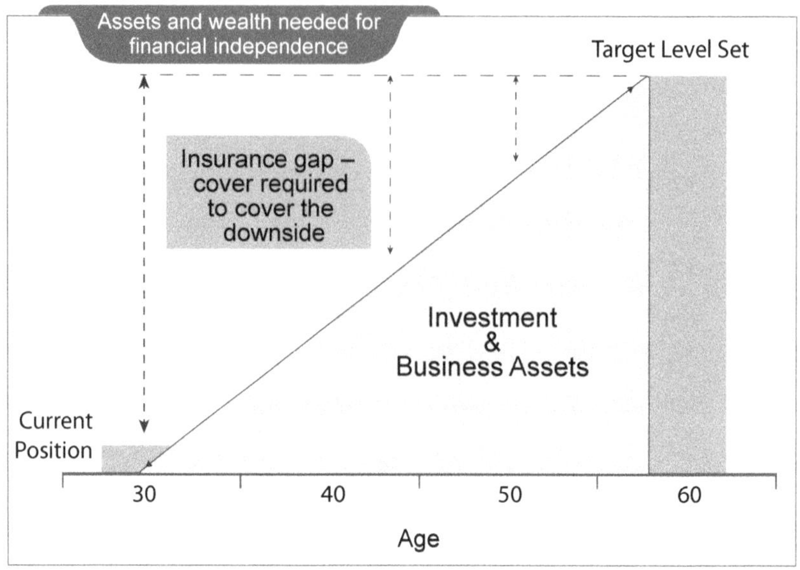

As this chart shows, the target level set reflects the investment and income-producing assets needed to retire or become financially independent, with enough income to fund your lifestyle. The gap between the value of your current income-producing assets and the assets you need is your downside risk. If, for example, you became very ill and could not work, this gap would hurt you financially. In simple terms, this is the gap you need to cover and insurance is a proven, cost-effective way to do this.

Whilst we all hope this never happens to us, covering this downside allows us to get on with our lives without worry of financial ruin or hardship.

Expense

The out-of-pocket costs for increasing your current insurance cover depends on certain variables, including but not limited to the types and levels of cover desired, your age, medical history, lifestyle, occupation risks, and, naturally, the various policy features and options. Generally speaking, the better the features, the more

　　　　　　　　　　　　　　　　Peter Gialouris

expensive the cover. For example, with income protection cover, the waiting period from the time income ceases due to sickness or injury until benefits are available affects the policy cost. Waiting periods typically range anywhere from 14 days up to two years, and the shorter the waiting period, the higher the premium.

The number of years you are eligible for benefits also affects the overall policy cost. The usual benefit periods are two years, five years, and up to age 70. Longer benefit periods generally feature higher premiums. Note that the cost of premiums are often reduced if paid annually, in advance.

Stepped- and Level-Premiums

Under the level-premium option, you pay a fixed premium throughout the life of the policy, while the stepped-premium option features a premium cost that increases over time, as your risk of claiming increases with age. With the level-premium option, to offset the fact that premium prices don't increase, you pay a higher annual premium from day one than you would with the stepped-level option. Note that your insurer may adjust both level- and stepped-premiums from time to time, up or down, in response to changing costs and market forces.

Tax-Deductible Insurance Premiums

In general, insurance premiums payable on life, TPD, and critical illness/trauma policies are not tax-deductible when implemented outside the superannuation structure. However, life and TPD insurance held within the superannuation structure may be partially, or in some instances completely, deductible to the fund. In addition, the insurance premiums can usually be funded through tax-deductible contributions if you are self-employed, or out of employer contributions – SGC or Salary Sacrifice* – made to your superannuation fund where your business is a company and you are its employee.

Generally, income protection and business expenses insurance premiums are tax-deductible.

** Note: Sacrificing pre-tax salary into superannuation is a simple and tax-effective way to increase superannuation benefits and decrease assessable income. Rather than receiving salary taxable at your marginal rate, you may arrange with your 'employer' (ie, your company) to forego part of your future wages or salary in exchange for receiving benefits of an equivalent amount. To be effective, any salary sacrifice arrangement between you and an employer for superannuation should be fully documented and must exist prior to the income being earned.*

Taxation of Benefits

Benefits paid on life, TPD, and critical illness/trauma policies outside superannuation are generally not subject to tax. When life cover is held within superannuation, the benefit is tax-free to financial dependants. (This is not necessarily tax-free to beneficiaries who are not financial dependants.) If the benefit is taken as an income stream, the income tax treatment is predicated on the age of the deceased at the time of death and the age of the beneficiary.

Tax liability on TPD benefits taken as a lump sum is dependent upon the age of the recipient and can include an additional tax-free component equal to the future service portion of the total benefit. If the monies are taken as a pension, beneficiaries under the age of 60 will receive a 15% offset on the taxable portion of the benefit.

Income payments made on income protection and business expenses insurance policies are included in your assessable income and taxed accordingly.

This table and matrix may prove helpful to gauge which types of insurance and items to cover to ensure you have adequate and comprehensive coverage.

Cover Needs	Types of Cover													
	Life	Income	TPD	Trauma	Medical	Building	Contents	Travel	Professional Indemnity	Public Liability	Business Expenses	Key Person	Buy Sell	Other
Personal														
Funeral	Y													
Medical		Y	Y	Y	Y			Y						
Mortgage	Y		Y	Y										
Other Loans	Y		Y	Y										
Funds for Children's Education	Y	Y	Y	Y										
Living Expenses	Y	Y	Y	Y										
Funds for Retirement	Y	Y	Y											
Property						Y	Y							
Other								Y		Y				Y
Business														
Property						Y	Y							
Business Expenses											Y			
Business Profits												Y		Y
Business Value												Y	Y	
Potential Liability									Y	Y				
Other								Y						Y
You Inc.	Y	Y	Y	Y	Y	Y	Y	Y	Y	Y	Y	Y	Y	Y
Relevant Provider*	P	P	P	P	G	G	G	G	G	G	G/P	P	P	G/P

*P = personal insurance specialist or qualified financial planner; G = general insurance specialist or broker

To calculate your overall insurance shortfall, use this worksheet.

Cover Needs	Types of Cover			
	Life You/ Partner	Income You/ Partner	TPD You/ Partner	Trauma You/ Partner
Payment of funeral expenses	$			
A lump sum to cover medical costs and expenses incurred to modify your car and home			$	$
Repayment of outstanding debts.	$		$	$
A capital lump sum, which, when invested at a projected conservative average rate of return, will provide the annual income your family requires, indexed for inflation.	$		$ (Income protection preferred)	$ (Income protection preferred)
Monthly benefit income protection benefit – maximum available		$		
A capital lump sum, which, when invested at a projected conservative average rate of return, indexed for inflation, for the years required to cover the shortfall in income between your current net income and the proposed income protection insurance.			$	$
A capital lump sum, which, when invested at a projected conservative average rate of return, will provide sufficient annual amount for your children, ages kindergarten to year 12, and possibly cover university education costs.	$		$	$

Cover Needs	Types of Cover			
	Life You/ Partner	Income You/ Partner	TPD You/ Partner	Trauma You/ Partner
Total Cover Required (A)				
Less:				
Superannuation	$		$	
Realisable assets	$		$	$
Net investment income		$		
Existing insurance cover to be retained	$	$	$	$
Total Investment Assets and Existing Insurance (B)	$	$	$	$
Additional cover required (A-B)	$	$	$	$

A financial planner or personal insurance specialist can offer you guidance on the level of cover you need.

Insurance protects you and your family. Why run the risk? You have enough business and financial issues without letting an injury, sickness or disruption to your business bring you down. I know of a business that was forced to close for a lengthy period because the property development next door resulted in subsidence, which caused the business's building to partially collapse. There was no way the business could have foreseen that happening. Insurance against loss of business profits protects you in these types of instances. Don't take chances. Insure yourself, and your livelihood, against the unexpected.

Key Points

- Risk management should be a factor in every business and investment decision you make.

- Consult an insurance specialist to identify potential gaps in cover and unnecessary risks you might face.

- Some insurance premiums may be tax-deductible. An advisor can show you how to best structure this.

Source: Many of the insurance definitions, technical material and the Insurance cover worksheet used in this section were provided by Lifespan Financial Planning Pty Ltd.

11

E: Estate and Succession Planning

Succession planning is easy to overlook or put off until tomorrow. The problem is what happens when tomorrow arrives and you haven't yet prepared. Succession planning is critical for small business owners who are often intrinsic to their business's success. Have you trained someone to step into your shoes on a moment's notice?

Consider a Sydney cake shop that offered superb quality baked goods. People came from all over the city to buy their biscuits and cakes. The owner's skill and intellectual property (secret recipes) were widely lauded as the main ingredients for the shop's success.

Then, disaster struck. Without warning, the owner fell ill. The family tried to help out, but they did not realise or appreciate the exceptional knowhow and talent involved in making these biscuits and cakes. Quality suffered and business rapidly declined. The business, now struggling, was sold for a drastically discounted percentage of its peak value.

The family's primary asset and bulk of their net worth all but disappeared. Why? Because the owner, a busy small business owner, was highly invested in the business and failed to take the time to put a simple succession plan in place.

Building a robust business is only part of what makes you successful. Having a solid succession plan in place provides you with a more saleable business, as well as a solid exit strategy when the time is right.

Business succession planning and a personal estate plan make up the last of the 6 Pillars, and, like risk management, are wealth-protecting strategies. The benefits of careful planning and the correct drafting and execution of these legal documents cannot be over-emphasised. The main purpose is to ensure that upon your retirement, disability or death, transfer of ownership or control of your assets is made to the appropriate person or entity at the right time and in the most effective manner.

Estate planning for a business owner is not without complexities, the goal being to achieve the optimum outcome as simply as possible, at minimum cost. It is advisable to work with a qualified professional to ensure you cover all the bases.

Succession Plan

A business succession plan is a key business management and protection strategy, but it can be a challenge to put in place effectively for a small business. However, it is worth the effort for a number of reasons.

- **It makes good business sense** – If you, the owner, or a key staff member is out of action, you have a plan to cover that gap and keep the business wheels turning.
- **It forms part of your exit strategy** – For a small business owner, a pre-planned internal buyout or external sale option sets your succession plan and exit strategy so the business can successfully continue after you retire or exit the business. The idea being that the business, and its value, does not solely rest with you being there to work your magic. Instead, you have developed a team and put systems in place that add value and make your business more marketable.

- **It helps with longer-term planning** – A plan to enable you, the owner, to step back from or sell the business, and the related financial and tax planning consequences, need to be considered and decisions made. Depending on the business, it can take as many as ten years to get this right, especially if your business relies on you too much right now.

- **It forms part of your estate plan** – At a minimum, the formal control of the business needs to be considered so decisions can be made if the owner is out of action (which may involve an Enduring Power of Attorney). If the business uses a company structure, the remaining directors have control of the company. Therefore, a new or alternate director to cover the owner needs to be considered and addressed.

A number of years ago, I learned of a successful business that sold shirts and school wear. The owner was 50 or 60 years old, loved the business, and had no desire to retire. However, he started to experience health problems and the business struggled as a result. His energy and drive were key to the success of the business. He was eventually forced to sell his business, when sales and profits dropped by 75%.

Owner health issues, losing the passion for the business, and experiencing burnout are common yet often unanticipated challenges business owners face. Putting in place a succession plan, and exit strategy, systems, and procedures to make the business less dependent on the owner should be your aim. This also takes pressure off you, as the owner, to do the bulk of the work and drive the business. It also improves the value of the business and makes it more saleable.

There are risks in doing this and they need to be managed, such as customers being poached when a key staff person leaves, or if initially the quality of the service is not as good as when you do the work yourself. You need to step up and be more of a teacher, coach, and manager to key staff.

It does not pay to put this in the 'too hard' basket. Not having a succession plan and linking this to your exit strategy leaves you exposed. It can have adverse consequences and come back to bite you.

Your Exit Strategy

Many years ago I had the floorboards sanded in my house. The contractor I used had an excellent reputation that was well deserved. However, he had chosen an apprentice who did not share his passion for the business. The apprentice was often late or failed to show up when scheduled and simply shrugged when confronted about it.

If the business owner had given serious thought to handing over his business when he was ready to retire, which admittedly was still some years away, he could have been grooming an eager successor who would effectively free him from the need to constantly supervise in order for his business to continue to succeed. A natural successor and buyer for the business could be developed if he had simply viewed an apprentice as a part of his future rather than an assistant for the here and now. He chose to stand still instead of move forward.

Succession Plan versus Exit Strategy

A succession plan can be a short-term remedy for when the business's key operator is absent or temporarily out of action, is promoted or leaves. It incorporates training and developing one or more persons to assume a key role to ensure the business continues smoothly, without interruption or a drop in customer service. It can be a longer term plan too.

A succession plan may or may not involve someone who is buying into the business to ensure a smooth transition that lowers the risk

Peter Gialouris

of a business subsequently losing value after transfer. In contrast, an exit strategy is a long-term plan that targets a permanent transition.

Generally, to maximise the sale price, you need to reduce the dependence of your business on you so that a buyer is assured that business will continue and that value will not be lost as a result.

The succession plan and business exit strategy are an important component of your overall business plan, and take into consideration the protection of your IP (intellectual property, such as proprietary designs, methods or, as in the case of the bakery, secret recipes), your customer base, and the goodwill your successful business generates. While sharing your proprietary secrets with another is not without risk, ignoring a succession plan to avert disaster or simply protect your business asset is arguably riskier.

Tax Advantages

Minimising the effect of capital gains tax when you sell your business should be a part of your overall strategy. How detailed this plan needs to be depends on how close you are to selling.

It is important to grasp just how capital gains are calculated and know the various ways you can maximise your cost base in order to minimise your tax liability. Always keep accurate, meticulous records. Work with your tax accountant/tax agent on this from the start, ideally even before you start your business.

Make sure you know how CGT will be calculated in your particular situation. Will you be taxed on the entire gain at your individual marginal tax rate? Does the general CGT discount on capital gains apply? At the time of writing, Australia grants most taxpayers (See: previous tax strategies chapter) a 50% discount on CGT if you have held the asset for more than 12 months.

You also need to learn what small business tax concessions apply, which are too numerous and nuanced to list here. Because this area is so complex, many small business owners fail to take advantage of these concessions, which are there precisely to benefit them. Some of these concessions can significantly reduce CGT or eliminate it entirely. Why would you want to give away your hard-earned profits?

Being able to preserve these net capital gains may also enable you to contribute more into your super for retirement. Plus, there are rollover provisions that can be useful when buying a new business. Ask your tax agent about which provisions offer you the best outcome.

As you get closer to selling, you will want to be more precise and detailed in your planning, to get specific advice on the capital gains you stand to earn, the potential concessions you can utilise, and the estimated CGT you may have to pay. Armed with this information, you can make more intelligent decisions as to how to manage the sale to enable you to build up your super nest egg or reinvest the proceeds, or both.

A succession plan provides you with the following benefits:

1. **Backup for key roles** – Keeps the doors open and the business running when you can't be there
2. **A more robust business** – Enables the business to cope with unfortunate events in the short term and reduce overall owner dependence
3. **A well thought out exit strategy** – Enhances the value of your business while reducing your risk

Personal Estate Plan

Your personal estate plan can address a lot of the financial fallout when things go wrong. Although some find it painful and confronting to think about, the pain and worry will only get worse if this is not properly addressed.

Your estate plan should always be up to date and in order, and include the following components:

- Last Will and Testament
- Death Benefit Nomination for Your Super
- Life Insurance Policies
- Enduring Power of Attorney (EPOA)
- Second-in-command (2IC)
- Enduring Guardianship
- Advance Care Plan/Advance Care Directive

Last Will and Testament

Your Will ensures that in the event of your death, your assets are distributed to your nominated beneficiaries. Circumstances change, so review your Will at least every two to three years, and make any necessary updates, to ensure it remains current. This can simply mean re-reading it to confirm it accurately reflects your wishes.

Note that any assets within your superannuation fund do not form part of your Will unless you have nominated your estate as the sole beneficiary. (See further below, regarding 'Death Benefit Nomination for Your Super' for more information). Additionally, jointly held assets, including bank accounts, insurance payouts, and possibly the family home (where it is jointly owned), lie outside the dictates of your Will.

Should you die without leaving a Will (referred to as dying intestate), the legal headaches and expenses you leave in your wake can be debilitating, even disastrous. The beneficiaries you may assume will be taken care of could be left without a penny. Is that what you want? Death is inevitable, but the care of your loved ones in your absence is not. If you have not done so already, contact a qualified estate planner or attorney and prepare one immediately.

Death Benefit Nomination for Your Super

The assets within your superannuation fund do not form part of your Will unless you have nominated your estate as the sole beneficiary of your super. In general, the trustees of your fund have the ultimate discretion to decide who receives your superannuation benefits, unless you make a binding death benefit nomination.

Where there is only a non-binding death benefit nomination, your superannuation fund beneficiary nominations are used solely as a guide. Again, the trustees of your fund have the final say in who receives your superannuation benefits.

However, if your superannuation fund allows you to make a *binding* death benefit nomination, the trustees must pay out your superannuation benefits to your nominated beneficiary, a dependant or dependants of your choice, or the person who is your legal personal representative. Some super funds feature a non-lapsing death benefit nomination, meaning that the binding death benefit nomination you make will never expire unless it's changed prior to your death; otherwise, binding death benefit nominations are only valid for three years and must be renewed at the end of that period.

Check your super fund to determine what death benefit nomination options you have.

If you would like another party, such as an adult child, friend or charity to receive your accumulated superannuation funds, consider nominating your estate as the preferred beneficiary of your superannuation entitlements and make this bequest a part of your

Will. Your superannuation will then be distributed according to the terms of your Will. This strategy may also enable you to minimise tax payable on the death benefits.

If your super is a self-managed super fund, with a company trustee, or if you have a company, or trust structure, determine whether the trustee or company director is legally permitted to act alone or whether two or more directors are required to make a decision and how it may affect the ability to carry out your wishes efficiently.

Life Insurance Policies

Unless you own the policy or have nominated your estate as the beneficiary of your life insurance policy, the proceeds will not form part of your Will.

It is important to note that jointly held assets, i.e., assets in joint names, pass onto the surviving owner. As noted above, they lie outside the scope of your Will. You cannot bequeath your share of the asset to an individual other than the person(s) owning it jointly with you.

In contrast, where the asset, such as a home or investment property, is owned as 'tenants in common', you each possess a specific percentage or share of the asset. Your share of the asset can be disbursed according to the dictates of your Will.

Enduring Power of Attorney (EPOA)

Should you become disabled or lose the capacity to make competent decisions, this document will provide your nominated attorney (usually a close relative or friend) the power to act on your behalf to manage your financial and legal affairs, including operating your bank account, paying bills, and selling and purchasing assets.

The only legal step they cannot take on your behalf is to draft and execute your Will.

There are two types of Power of Attorney, the standard, which is a temporary appointment, and an Enduring Power of Attorney, which ensures that your nominated attorney retains the power to act on your behalf if you suffer a loss of capacity through unsoundness of mind.

You may be familiar with Michael Schumacher, the Formula One racing champion, and his life-threatening skiing accident in 2013. He suffered severe head injuries, spent months in an induced coma, and needed years of care and treatment. How would your business and affairs be managed if you experienced such a disaster? An Enduring Power of Attorney looks after your affairs in just such a situation. An estate-planning specialist can best advise you on what is best for your situation.

Second-in-Command (2IC)

When you run a business, you need a second-in-command who can step into your shoes in the event you are disabled or simply as part of your exit strategy. This requires identifying the most ideal person you feel confident can assume your role in a way that ensures that your business will continue to run as it does now, under your leadership. Benefits of this include not just your peace of mind but maintaining the valuation of your business should it be sold down the road.

Enduring Guardianship

An Enduring Guardianship is similar to an Enduring Power of Attorney, but in this instance, you appoint one or more persons to, either jointly or separately, to make lifestyle, health, and medical decisions for you when you are not capable of doing this for yourself.

(Should you later recover your ability to make decisions, the Enduring Guardianship automatically becomes void.) Your enduring guardian may make decisions such as where you live (your home versus a care facility, for example), what services are provided to you at home, and what medical treatment you receive.

Enduring Guardianship and Enduring Power of Attorney documents are complementary and can be created separately, or as one document should you wish to appoint the same person to assume both responsibilities.

If you fail to appoint an enduring guardian and your doctor has not identified a 'person responsible' who they feel has a substantial enough connection to you personally to agree to or refuse treatment on your behalf, in NSW an application will be made to the Guardianship Division, NSW Civil & Administrative Tribunal, to appoint a guardian for you. If no one suitable is available to be your guardian, the tribunal may appoint an independent public official, a public guardian, who will make the necessary decisions regarding where you live, how you will be cared for, and even who may visit you.

Advance Care Plan/Advance Care Directive

These documents, which do not require the signature of a witness, establish your wishes to guide your enduring guardian when difficult choices must be made, such as whether to continue life support or whether you prefer all forms of treatment be provided to you to sustain life or just certain ones (extraordinary life-prolonging measures, or blood transfusions vs. palliative care, i.e., medications and pain relief, administering food and water, etc.) Taking the time to draft these documents goes a long way to easing the pain of a loved one having to make such critical decisions on your behalf.

Estate Plan Considerations

As you can see from the above components of your estate plan, while it will inevitably be a difficult situation within your business and for your family, you can ease the pain if you plan ahead and have most of your affairs in order and dealt with if anything happens to you. It is beneficial, when developing or reviewing your estate plan, to consider the following possibilities with regard to your beneficiaries:

- **Financial mismanagement risk** – This is a concern where a beneficiary is not good with money, such as through lack of experience, discipline or addiction, such as a gambling or drug habit. You may want to consider appointing a trustee.
- **Bankruptcy/creditor risk** – This is where your beneficiary is at financial risk. Would you want their inheritance to go straight to their creditors?
- **Spouse/divorce risk** – You may wish to avoid the risk that if a beneficiary's marriage breaks up, the ex-spouse takes half of the inheritance, or that it might go to the ex-spouse's children from another relationship.
- **Tax payable on distribution** – Some estate distributions are tax-free, whilst others may be taxable. It generally depends on the source of the distributions and who the beneficiary is. For example, the family home is tax exempt, whilst the payment of super death benefits to non-dependants may involve tax liability.

Who to Trust

Choosing who you wish to fulfil the roles of executor, attorney and guardian are not decisions to be made lightly. You want someone who is decisive, whom you trust to follow your wishes and have your best interest at heart. In particular, if you choose to appoint joint persons, consider the possibility of them disagreeing and how you might best avoid stalemate positions. I often recommend to clients to include a 'circuit breaker' in the event that parties disagree, such as appointing an odd number of trusted people, where the majority rules. Think about whether it would be best to have a non-loved one as part of the team, such as your accountant, lawyer or a professional trustee.

The above risks should be considered when drafting your estate plan. There are measures you can take to minimise such risks. It is wise to be specific and allow for flexibility. Trying to 'rule from the grave' can result in unintended consequences. When in doubt, keep it simple, and stick to proven and established practices. An estate-planning specialist is a valuable asset when creating your estate plan as a business owner.

Align the Business and Personal

Many small business owners do not grasp how important it is to ensure that business and personal plans for the future work together. Let's look at one example.

Say you own a business and a number of trucks. You do not want your spouse to be burdened with the trucks if something happened to you, so you insert a clause in your Will that states that all trucks go to your brother or close friend, someone who perhaps is in a similar business and would benefit from them more. However, you operate your business through a company and *your company owns the trucks.*

In your Will, your shares in the company pass onto your spouse. So, although it was not your intent to leave the trucks to your spouse, because the company owns the trucks, your spouse ends up with them anyway, and the clause leaving them to another beneficiary is deemed void.

Your business and its structures (company, trust, etc.) all need careful consideration in your Will. This is where an estate-planning specialist can help.

These key areas can add value and make life easier if they are aligned including:

- Control of your business, your estate plan, and your Enduring Power of Attorney (EPOA)
- Your Will and the treatment of your business
- Succession plan and risk management when the owner or key staff are out of action
- Exit strategy and your retirement plan
- How your estate plan relates to insurance policies, your superannuation, and any related tax consequences

Key Points

- Succession and estate planning are often overlooked or pushed to the back burner until disaster strikes – by then it's too late.

- Knowing you have a plan in place when something happens that prevents you from working is the ultimate peace of mind, especially if you have family or others depending on you.

- A succession plan is part of your exit strategy – ensuring that the business remains viable and successful even (and especially) when you're not there. That protects you both in emergency situations and when you decide to sell.

- Capital gains tax planning should be an integral part of your strategy.

- Don't be squeamish – if you don't have a Last Will & Testament, an Enduring Power of Attorney, Enduring Guardianship, a Death Benefit Nomination for Your Super, and Life Insurance in place, do it now – today!

Source: Many of the definitions and technical material referred to in this chapter were provided by Lifespan Financial Planning Pty Ltd or in the case of the Enduring Guardianship and Advanced Care Directive sourced from the NSW Trustee & Guardian website © State of New South Wales (NSW Trustee & Guardian).

Section 4

Gain an Edge

12

The Value of Professional Advice

Small business owners have their hands full, with limited resources and never enough help. Getting good advice in the gap areas can mean the difference between operating a well-oiled machine and one that is neglected. Advisors include accountants, lawyers, financial advisors/planners, bankers, insurance brokers, business coaches, mentors, and business specialists.

Even advisors benefit from specialist advice. When I was in my late twenties, I received a partnership offer from my employer, an accounting firm. I was married, with one child and another on the way. We had a house with a mortgage and money was tight. The offer of partnership was a huge honour, and the potential success it portended seemed a dream come true.

Because I worked in the business and knew the partners, staff and clients very well, it would have been easy to just accept, without doing my homework. But, as partnering in a firm was new to me, and a big step, there were a couple of technical points on partnership liability I wanted to confirm before I made a commitment. I jotted down some very specific questions, which I estimated could be answered in half an hour, tops, which would keep my consultation costs as low as possible.

I had used a solicitor to buy my house but he was not experienced enough on commercial legal issues, so I found a city lawyer who advertised having over 30 years' experience in these matters. That sounded good to me. With his experience, I reasoned, the meeting would be short and the fee affordable.

I arrived for my appointment with a one-page summary I had prepared and began running through the specific issues I wanted addressed, when he interrupted me.

Peter, I'm going to stop the clock. You will not be charged for this. I'd like to understand more about the background of this firm that has offered you a partnership.

He proceeded to list names of various accounting firms over the past 30 years that had plunged into financial difficulty, some of which went broke. Up to that point, I had never heard of accounting firms going broke. How could they go broke, I wondered? Surely all accounting firms make money – they're run by accountants!

He began asking me questions.

What are the financial positions of the partners? Do any have a lot of debt?

I had no idea, but I added that as I would only be their business partner, I would not be liable for their personal debts. He shook his head.

If they have financial difficulties and become bankrupt, the bankruptcy trustee will sell their assets. And one of those assets would invariably be their share in the partnership. If that happens, the remaining partners will either need to buy that partner's share or sell the practice.

That was a risk I had not considered. I made a note to check on it.

Tell me about the firm's professional indemnity insurance (PI) coverage. Will it cover you as a new partner for claims relating to matters before you became a partner?

I knew the firm had PI cover, but liability for pre-existing issues was something that hadn't occurred to me. I made a note to check on that as well.

How profitable is the firm, as a business?

I hesitated. I knew the clients I looked after were profitable, but I had never seen the full financials. He said that, in his experience, when someone is offered partnership to a legal or accounting firm, they get so caught up in the excitement of it that they forget this is a business decision too – they are buying into a business. I promised to get the financials. I was fairly confident the numbers would be good.

Have you – and your wife – prepared a Last Will & Testament?

I had mentioned I was married and had a family. He added that we needed to choose executors, and guardians for the children.

Needless to say, the meeting took a lot longer than half an hour. Despite my having prepared the technical legal points I wanted to cover, I had not anticipated the number of significant issues he raised. It proved an excellent investment.

As it turned out, one of the partners did have a high level of debt, and the firm's PI policy did not fully protect me against past claims – it was a little grey. And due to a recent relocation, the financials, which I only obtained after multiple requests, had not just existing red ink but forecasted red ink. In addition, one of the partners had decided to sell their share, which was why they needed a new partner to buy into the business, and possibly even kick in some extra funds.

Thanks to the sage advice from that experienced lawyer, who was worth every penny I paid, and more, and the issues that were subsequently uncovered, I elected to forego the partnership offer. And I wasted no more time arranging the preparation of Wills for both my wife and me, to protect our family.

The value of that experience was one of the reasons I decided to start my own practice and provide business and financial advice. It is also why I now focus on the value of the advice rather than the cost. It's important to spend time getting to know the client and their background in order to address both the issues they raise and the issues they may not realise they have.

If, when you bought your first car, no one ever told you that you needed to maintain it in order to keep it running – repeatedly fill the fuel tank, change the oil, maintain the other fluids and tyre pressure, for example – how could you expect it to run efficiently and consistently? Expert advice is as much about revealing issues you have not considered or are completely unaware of as reinforcing what you know or expand upon what you have identified already. When I sit down with a client, my job is to provide them that kind of value.

It is easy to procrastinate when it comes to planning for the future, but the future is just around the corner. I had a dear friend who would often say to me, 'I need to come and see you one of these days, to get my affairs in order'. I tried on a number of occasions to set up a meeting, but he never got around to it. One day he telephoned me and said he urgently needed my help. He had been diagnosed with a terminal illness and only had months to live. He looked after the financial matters for most of his family, including the paperwork.

I did what I could, but we needed considerably more time than he had left and he passed away before we could resolve everything. All we had managed was to essentially kick the can down the road, to make small improvements but which did not address all the issues. We needed more time to sort out all the issues and take things to a new level for the future. This is a lot harder and more time consuming, but unquestionably more beneficial in the long run.

As a result, the family was left to deal not only with the terminal illness and eventual loss of my friend but also the unresolved financial issues. It would have been a lot simpler, and a lot easier on his family, if we had started earlier, when things were far less complicated.

One mistake people make is to worry too much about the cost of the advice and not enough about the benefit or its long-term value. Another is to pick the wrong advisor.

I have never understood why some people would rather listen to the 'free' financial advice their neighbour hands out than pay to consult a financial expert. Picking the right advisor is critical. Would you ask an electrician to fix your toilet? Or ask your mechanic how to best set up a business plan? I was fortunate in the lawyer I chose. If we had stuck to the half-hour, narrow meeting agenda that I'd had in mind, I would have blindly gone ahead with the partnership offer, likely causing untold problems and rough times for my young family as well as me.

How do you know you are getting good advice? Get a second opinion. That is a good way to confirm the advice you have been given, especially if you have doubts as to whether the advisor has your best interests at heart.

> ### Tips to find the right advisor
>
> - Ask people you trust (friends, successful colleagues, other experts) for referrals.
> - Shop around. Talk to a number of advisors before you make up your mind. Check their experience, qualifications, and any references.
> - If you are not sure, try them out on a specific, small matter and then reassess it.
> - Beware of professional advisors who focus on selling you a product versus giving you good advice. Choose key questions designed to reveal this.
> - Focus on the value of the advice rather than the cost. You want value for money. The cheapest (or the dearest) may not be the advisor best suited to you and your needs.

Every small business owner needs a team of reliable advisors, willing to work when it matters – a good lawyer, a tax accountant, and an insurance and financial advisor, at minimum.

No matter how tempting it might seem to economise, you simply cannot do it all yourself, and run your business, and do it all right. You need good advice from trusted specialists. Tax is one good example. The tax rules are very complex and good tax advice can pay for itself many times over. The same can be said for good investment advice, legal advice, and many other forms of expert advice.

The advice you need depends to a great extent on what you want to achieve. A good advisor will always ask you that question at the start – *What are your goals?* You need to be clear on that. If you're not, your brains trust of advisors can help guide you and clarify your goals and objectives.

Key Points

- No one can be an expert, or objective, in all areas. Even experts benefit from expert advice.

- Don't make the mistake of prioritising the cost of the advice over the long-term value of the advice. The latter is always more important.

- Just as with health issues, if you're unsure about the advice you receive, always get a second opinion.

13

Go from a Maze to Amazing!

Walk the Talk

Over the years, I have helped put together some powerful business and personal financial action plans. Not all were fully implemented. The hardest thing can be to make the changes – to Walk the Talk.

You need to Walk the Talk, to take the necessary steps outlined in this book, to apply CADTRE, the 6 Pillars of Financial Success, to both your business and personal affairs, review it all regularly, and trust that the thinking and planning that you and your team have done has put you on the right track.

You're time poor. I get that. That's precisely why it is important to make time to establish your priorities and honour them, and then implement those changes designed to have a big or immediate positive impact. Don't be the hamster on the wheel, running and running and never getting anywhere.

Your Call to Action

Start today – right now. Choose to work *in, on* and *beyond* your business by taking control. How? By following CADTRE, the 6 Pillars of Financial Success and applying them to both your business and personal financial affairs.

1. Harness **C**ash flow
2. Build **A**ssets
3. Control **D**ebt
4. Minimise **T**ax
5. Cover downside **R**isks
6. Implement a tailored exit strategy and **E**state plan

Change the equation from *No Money + No Help + No Time = No Way Forward* to a better, more satisfying one:

More Money + More Help + More Time = A New Way Forward

Get your business humming and schedule time on your calendar to sit down every few months, or every year, to review the business and update your financial, succession, and estate plans.

The ultimate goal is to make you financially independent of your business. Establish a process, check your progress, have the catch-up meeting you need to make it happen, and stay on track. You are worth your time and effort.

No excuses.
No putting it off.
Just do it.
Own Your Plan!

Appendix A

Short Form Business and Personal Financial Plan

Your Business Plan

Year 1: ___________

Mission

____

____

____

Vision

____

____

____

Values

____

____

____

Goals/Objectives

1. ____

2. ____

3. ____

4. ____

5. ____

SWOT Analysis

Strengths	Weaknesses

Opportunities	Threats

Specific Actions and Plans – Strategies

Cost-Benefit Analysis

(Use one page for each separate analysis)

Proposed Action:

Associated Costs	Potential/Actual Benefits

Organisation Chart – Current and Planned
(Business Plan Only)

People and roles:

Annual Budget and Years 2 & 3 Projections
(Business Plan Only)

	Current	Year 1/ Budget	Year 2	Year 3
Sales				
Cost of Sales				
Gross Profit				
Gross Profit %				
Overheads				
Staff				
Rent				
Other Expenses				
Total Operating Expenses				
Net Profit				
Tax				
Net Profit After Tax				
Capital Expenditure				
Asset Disposals				
Other major items:				

Balance Sheet

(Business Plan Only)

	Current	Year 1/ Budget	Year 2	Year 3
Bank				
Trade Debtors				
Inventory				
GST Receivable				
Other Current Assets				
Total Current Assets				
Fixed Assets				
Total Assets				
GST Payable				
Trade Creditors				
Other Creditors				
Accruals				
Provisions				
Other current liabilities				
Total Current Liabilities				
Loans				
Total Non-Current Liabilities				
Total Liabilities				
Net Assets				

Cash Flow Report

(Business Plan Only)

	Current	Year 1/ Budget	Year 2	Year 3
Opening Bank				
+ Net profit after tax				
+ Depreciation				
- Capital expenditure				
+ Disposals				
+ Decrease (- Increase) in current assets				
+ Increase (- Decrease) in current liabilities				
+ Increase (- Decrease) in loans				
Other				
Net Cash flow				
Closing Bank				

Your Personal Financial Plan

Goals/Objectives

1. ____

2. ____

3. ____

4. ____

5. ____

Net Worth Calculation
(Personal Plan Only)

Asset	Current Market Value
Personal/Lifestyle Assets	
Home/Primary Residence	
House Contents	
Valuables (list individually)	
Car	
Additional Vehicles	
Caravan/Boat	
Holiday Home	
Other	
Total Lifestyle Assets	
Investments/Savings	
Cheque Account	
Savings/ Cash Management Accounts	
Term Deposits	
Rental Property	
Managed Funds	
Life Insurance Cash Value	
Net Business Value/Equity	
Super/Retirement Accounts	
Other	
Total Investment Assets	
TOTAL ASSETS	

Liability	Current Amount Owed
Primary Residence Mortgage	
Loan/Mortgage Offset Account	
Mortgages/Investment Loans on Other Properties	
Car Loan	
Personal Loans/Guarantees	
Credit Card Debt	
Student Loan	
Other Loans	
TOTAL LIABILITIES	

Total Assets – Total Liabilities = Net Worth: $__________________

Budget/Cash Flow Report
(Personal Plan Only)

	Current	Year 1	Year 2	Year 3
INCOME				
Salary/wages				
Business Income/Dividends				
Investment Income				
Other				
Income Tax Payable				
Medicare Levy Payable				
Net Income after tax				
EXPENSES				
Living/Lifestyle Expenses				
Housing (mortgage/ rent/ rates)				
Utilities (electric/gas/oil, water, rubbish, mobile and landline phones, TV/cable/ streaming video, internet)				
Food (groceries/ takeaway/eating out)				
Transport/travel(car, public transport, etc.)				
Insurance premiums				
Personal care (clothing, toiletries, grooming)				
Health/Medical (Doctor, Dentist, Chemist, etc)				

Peter Gialouris

	Current	Year 1	Year 2	Year 3
Pets (food, insurance, healthcare, grooming)				
Family (education, hobbies, childcare, tuition, child support, alimony)				
Personal debt (credit cards, personal loan payments)				
Investment Loan				
Investment Expenses				
Goal-oriented savings (e.g., emergency fund, retirement, vacation)				
Charitable Donations/ Gifts				
Other				
Total Expenses				
TOTAL NET CASH FLOW				

Key financial weaknesses, issues and gaps that need to be addressed

Specific Actions and Plans – Strategies

Cost-Benefit Analysis

(Use one page for each separate analysis)

Proposed Action:

Associated Costs	Potential/Actual Benefits

Are your Business and Personal Financial Plans Aligned?

Pillar	Business Plan Yes/No – Issue?	Personal Plan Yes/No – Issue?	Action Required
Cash flow			
Assets			
Debt			
Tax			
Risk			
Estate Plan			

Appendix B
Business and Investment Structures

See facing table

Feature	Individual/ Sole Trader	Partnership/ Joint Ownership	Company	Discretionary Trust	Unit Trust	SMSF
Legal Status	Individual	Partners	Separate Legal Entity	Trustee responsible	Trustee responsible	Trustee responsible
Asset Protection	None	None	Liability can be limited to company assets.	Liability can be limited to Trust assets.	Liability can be limited to Trust assets.	Liability can be limited to Super Fund assets.
Income Tax	Marginal Tax Rates (MTR) of the individual.	Marginal Tax Rates (MTR) of the Partners.	Company Tax rate. Franked dividends can pass the company tax paid, onto the shareholders, reducing their tax.	Marginal Tax Rates (MTR) of the beneficiaries.	Marginal Tax Rates (MTR) of the Unit Holders.	Valuable concessional tax rates apply in the accumulation and pension phases.
Capital Gains Tax (CGT)	Asset held more than 12 months benefits from a CGT discount.	Asset held more than 12 months - CGT discount applies.	No CGT discount.	Asset held more than 12 months - CGT discount applies.	Asset held more than 12 months - CGT discount applies.	Valuable concessional tax rates apply in the accumulation and pension phases.
Accumulate Earnings	No	No	Yes	No	No	Yes for Members
Tax Losses	Included in Tax Return	Included in Tax Return of the Partners	Can't distribute losses to shareholders.	Can't distribute losses to beneficiaries.	Can't distribute losses to Unit Holders.	Generally allocated to the Members.

Feature	Individual/ Sole Trader	Partnership/ Joint Ownership	Company	Discretionary Trust	Unit Trust	SMSF
Transfers on death	By Will	Depends on the Partnership Agreement or if tenants in common (By Will) or joint ownership (Surviving partner).	Shares held depends on the Shareholder's Will.	Depends on Trust Deed	Units held - depends on Trust Deed and Unit Holder's Will.	Binding Death Benefit Nomination or Trustee discretion and the Fund Trust Deed.
Costs		Some additional costs but less than a company or a Trust	Costs to set up and maintain	Costs to set up and maintain. Can be more than a company structure.	Costs to set up and maintain. Can be more than a company structure.	Costs to set up and maintain. Generally more than a Company or a normal Trust.
Suitability	Most simple businesses where asset protection is not as important.	Jointly owned property or most simple businesses.	Most businesses. Can be tax effective and provide asset protection benefits.	Families or family businesses where asset protection, income distribution and flexibility is important.	Investments where specific entitlements and asset protection is important.	Where asset protection, owning the business premises and flexibility and control over your super is important.

Crafting an Investment Strategy

See table over page

Attributes

Attribute	Cash	Fixed Interest/Bonds	Shares	Property	Alternative investments	
Tax benefits	N	N	Y	Y	Part	Part
Inflation Protection	N	N	Y	Y	Part	Part
Low Volatility	Y	Yes for quality	N	N	N	N
Diversification	Y	Y	Y	Part	Part	Part
Depth of Market	Y	Y	Y	Y	Part	Part
Capital security	Y	Yes for quality	Part	Part	N generally	Part
Divisibility	Y	Y	Y	N	Part	Part
Liquidity	Y	Yes for quality	Yes for quality	N	Low	Part
Growth	N	Low	Y	Y	Part	Part
Income	Y	Y	Y	Y	Part	Part

Features

Cash - The capital is safe relative to other asset classes. You have immediate access to your funds.

Fixed Interest/Bonds - Generally secure. Income is known.

Shares - Growth above inflation in the long term. Growing income. Potential for tax benefits. Easily cashed in. Easy to divide up the assets. Can diversify internationally. Can reinvest via dividend plans.

Property - Capital value and income should rise with inflation. Potential for tax benefits. Emotional security of *bricks and mortar*.

Alternative investments are a non-homogeneous group. These assets can be commodities, natural resources, private equity and venture capital. These strategies generally show very low correlation to the returns of traditional portfolios

Features	Income	Growth	Liquidity	Divisibility	Capital security	Depth of Market	Diversification	Low Volatility	Inflation Protection	Tax benefits
Overall - Number of asset classes with this attribute	4	2	3	3	2	4	4	2	2	2
Cash	Y	N	Y	Y	Y	Y	Y	Y	N	N
Fixed Interest	Y	N	Y	Y	Y	Y	Y	Y	N	N
Property	Y	Y	N	N	N	Y	Y	N	Y	Y
Shares	Y	Y	Y	Y	N	Y	Y	N	Y	Y
Australian Shares	Y	Y	Y	Y	N	Y	Y	N	Y	Y
Overseas shares	Less so	Y	Y	Y	N	Y	Y	N	Y	Y

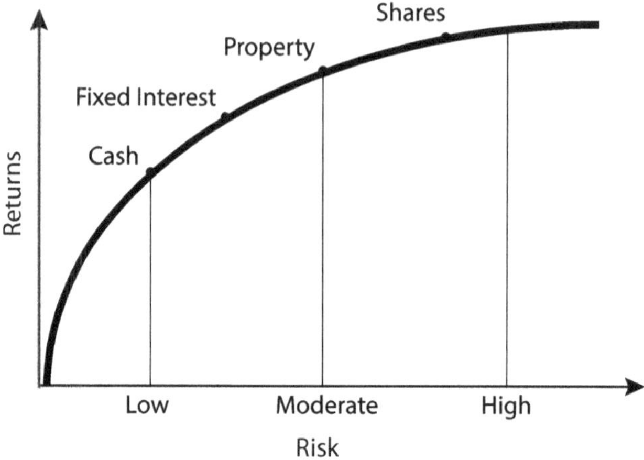

Source: Lifespan Financial Planning Pty Ltd.

The graph above shows the return and risk relationship of the above key 4 investment sectors or asset classes. It also depicts the need for the higher risk asset classes to achieve a higher return. Otherwise, if investment risk is not rewarded in the long term, then the investment return of the more secure asset classes like cash and bonds will drop. That is, this investment money has nowhere to go. No one would borrow money to invest in property and businesses (shares) if the reward was not there. However, the asset classes with higher risk are more volatile in the short term. Generating potentially higher returns and poor returns and losses during a downturn. The table below quantifies the expected longer-term returns and the historical variance in those returns of the key assets classes. These returns can be significantly affected by inflation.

                     Peter Gialouris

Expected Long-Term Average Gross Income & Growth for Individual Asset Classes

Asset Class	Working Long-Term Gross Returns[1]			Historical Annual Return Volatility[2]	
	Income %	Growth %	Total Return %	Annual Return Variance multiple (+ or -)	Comments, General Factors and Key Influences
Australian Shares	4	5	9	> 5 times	Sector, interest rates and inflation
International Shares	2	7	9	> 5 times	Country, foreign currency (hedged/unhedged), sector, interest rates and inflation
Property Securities	6	2	8	> 5 times	Sector, location, interest rates, inflation, gearing, whether the property/security is listed/unlisted, or a development/established
Australian Fixed Interest	5	1	6	> 2 times	Credit risk, investment grade, interest rates and inflation
International Fixed Interest	5	1	6	> 2 times	Country, foreign currency (hedged/unhedged), credit risk, investment grade, interest rates and inflation
Cash	5	0	5	> 1 times	Inflation
Inflation (CPI)			3	> 1 times	Can be negative. High inflation rates have been more common in the past, including rates over 10% in the 1970's and 1980's

1 Lifespan Financial Planning Pty Ltd. Please note that these income and growth rates are based on projected future performance, and are intended only as a guide to likely returns over the medium to long term (over 5 years) and should be treated with caution.

2 Review of relevant market indices, (ASX, MSCI etc.) as well as the Author's own experience over the last 40 years, including the 1987 stock market crash, Australian recession and commercial property market crash (early 1990's), Asian Currency Crisis (late 1990's), the dot.com bubble (late 1990's/early 2000's), September 11 (2001) and the GFC (Global Financial Crisis 2007-2008).

The variance multiple above refers to how much higher (or lower) past annual returns over the last 40 years have been compared to the working L.T. total return in this table for the relevant asset class. e.g. Australian shares – annual gains greater than 54% and annual losses greater than 36% have occurred. Similar variances have also occurred for international shares and property. Bonds and cash have been volatile too, but less so.

Recommended Reading

John McGrath, *You inc.: How to attract amazing success into your life and business*, HarperCollins Publishers (Australia), 2003

Michael E. Gerber, *The E-Myth Revisited,* HarperCollins Publishers, 1995

George S. Clason, *The Richest Man in Babylon*, Penguin Publishing Group, 2002

NSW Trustee & Guardian: www.tag.nsw.gov.au

About the Author

I grew up in Weethalle, a little town in country New South Wales, Australia – what people often refer to as a one-horse town. There was more than one horse, but you get the picture.

Small towns are the birthplace of small businesses. Each town has its own story. Most have a War Memorial. Whenever you pass near one, drop in. Buy a drink or a bite to eat. Take a look at their war contribution and sacrifice. It always touches the heart. The businesses need, and welcome, your passing trade.

I worked in the family business, originally a rest stop café catering for passing trade, back as far as I can remember. I learnt how to balance the till at the end of the day and the importance of banking the takings. I learnt about the back office part of the business, and that this needs to be done well. I learnt that a cheque is nothing more than a piece of paper unless you have money in the bank to back it.

Over time, the focus of the business became one of a general store catering for the locals, bringing in fresh produce to the townspeople and farmers. This proved a better business model than simply a café.

As soon as I could read and write, I helped write letters asking for a refund or a credit on a supplier's account. Virtually every letter ended with 'Please give us a credit' (i.e. adjust for the overcharge or short shipment etc). To this day, I am not sure if those letters I laboured over were sent or whether my father just wanted to teach me how to write them.

I was less comfortable with the front office, serving the customers. Initially, I had to stand on a box to see over the counter.

One day, a woman from one of the local farms came in with her children, some of whom I went to school with. Back then we still used imperial weights – ounces, pounds, and stones.

The shop scales could only weigh up to four pounds. When she asked for six pounds of tomatoes, I panicked. 'The scales only go up to four pounds,' I blurted out. She gave me a puzzled look and then smiled. 'I'll take four pounds of tomatoes then,' she said. Relieved, I weighed and handed her four pounds of tomatoes and told her the price. She nodded and paid for them. 'I'll take two pounds of tomatoes now,' she said. The penny dropped. Lesson learnt.

When I was 15, my parents sold the business and moved us to the big smoke of Sydney, to ensure their seven children had access to better education and job opportunities. It was the early 1970s, when inflation was high and times were getting tough. It was my first experience with a business exit.

I grew up to become an accountant, working for professional accounting firms and in commerce, with large and small businesses of all sizes, types, and industries.

These days I run my own business, focusing on business consulting and financial planning. I work primarily with business owners and enjoy helping them achieve a level of financial success and independence they never dreamt they could manage. That success is why I wrote this book. As a small business owner, this book is for you. I hope you find it useful.

Peter Gialouris
CADTRE Consulting

Contact the author at:

www.cadtre.com.au

peter.gialouris@cadtre.com.au